Kids can
Quilt

3-06

Kids can Quilt

Fun and easy projects for your small quilter

Dorothy Stapleton

BARRON'S

A QUARTO BOOK

First edition for North America published in 2004
by Barron's Educational Series, Inc.

All inquiries should be addressed to:
Barron's Educational Series, Inc.
250 Wireless Boulevard
Hauppauge, NY 11788

http://www.barronseduc.com

International Standard Book Number 0-7641-2770-5
Library of Congress Catalog Card Number 2003109117

QUAR.QFK

Conceived, designed, and produced by
Quarto Publishing plc
The Old Brewery
6 Blundell Street
London N7 9BH

Project Editor Paula McMahon
Senior Art Editor Sally Bond
Copy Editor Sarah Hoggett
Designer Julie Francis
Photographers Colin Bowling, Paul Forrester
Illustrator Coral Mula
Proof reader Jenny Siklós
Indexer Pamela Ellis

Art Director Moira Clinch
Publisher Piers Spence

Manufactured by PICA Digital, Singapore
Printed by Star Standard Industries (PTE) Ltd,
Singapore

9 8 7 6 5 4 3 2 1

Contents

Introduction

Quilting is fun and easy to do. If you can sew a few stitches, you can quilt. Even if you can't sew at all this book will show you how. So when the TV gets boring, why not start to quilt. There are lots of easy projects in this book and some will make great presents for all of the family.

Quilting is a very old tradition that has been handed down from mothers to daughters as a craft they can share and enjoy together. You might be lucky enough to have antique quilts in your family that were made by your grandmother or even your great-grandmother. It is also a very modern craft—quilters are always coming up with new ideas for things to make, and this book contains lots of fun projects—from little pincushions and pillows to pretty pictures in fabric— that you can make in just an hour or so.

In fact, that's one of the best things about quilting: it's so simple. If you can thread a needle and do a running stitch, you can already quilt—and if you can't do either of those things, this book will soon show you how! Everyone likes a homemade present, and many of the projects in this book make great gifts for your friends and family. For very little cost and effort, you can turn a worn-out piece of fabric

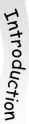

that most people would just throw away into something new and exciting. And, of course, there are so many lovely new materials on sale that you will have no problem finding inexpensive fabrics.

People who quilt find it a very relaxing hobby—but be warned: once you start to quilt, you'll find it's hard to put down a project until you've finished it! So enjoy the book and start quilting. Your friends will be impressed with your newfound quilting genius—and they'll never guess just how easy it really is!

Materials and equipment

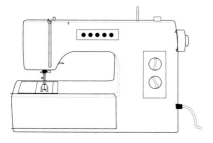

You may have to buy some pieces of equipment before you start quilting, but you will probably find that you already have a lot of the things that you need. This part of the book tells you what you will need.

It's a good idea to keep all your equipment together in a basket or box, so that you don't have to waste time looking for the things you need when you could be quilting. It will also keep your little brothers or sisters from "borrowing" your things!

Sewing machine

If your mom or grandmother has a sewing machine that you can use, that's great; if not, don't worry, because you can sew most of the projects in this book by hand.

If you are using a sewing machine, ask an adult to show you how it works. If the machine can work at a slow speed, ask to have it set like that. Some machines can do only straight and zigzag stitches, but others can do lots of fancy embroidery stitches. You can make up your own patterns with some machines, as they are computerized. Some machines can even do writing or repeat stitches that you have programmed into the machine.

If you're borrowing someone else's machine, always ask permission before you use it. Remember to return it to the stitch that you started with and to switch it off when you've finished using it.

Needles

There are different kinds of needles, and they all have different names. Some of the names sound a little strange! Medium-length, all-purpose needles are called "sharps," and shorter needles are called "betweens." You can also buy special quilting needles, which are short and can be very small. However, you don't need to use these: the shorter "betweens" needles will be fine.

Needles range in size from 1 to 10; the larger the number, the smaller the needle. It's best to start with a needle that has a big eye, as they are easier to thread. Size 6 or 7 is a good choice to begin with. When you get used to sewing and quilting, you will be able to use a smaller needle and therefore make smaller stitches. You can buy packets of different-sized needles, which are ideal if you are new to sewing.

Quilting   Betweens   Sharps

Pins

You need pins to hold pieces of fabric together. Any straight pins will do, but pins with colored glass heads are good, because they are easy to find when you drop them. (But once you've made the Ladybug Pincushion on pages 84–87, that won't be a problem!) Remember that pins and needles are very sharp— so if you have an inquisitive little brother or sister, keep the pins in a tin or box out of their way.

Safety pins are useful for pinning layers of fabric together before you quilt. (If you baste the layers together, the threads can get tangled up with your quilting stitches.) You can usually get safety pins free from the dry cleaners, as they pin labels to the clothes so that they know who they belong to.

Scissors

You can get scissors in various sizes; a medium-sized pair that is sharp enough for cutting fabric will be fine to start with. You will also need some paper-cutting scissors for some of the patterns. Don't cut paper with your fabric-cutting scissors, as it makes them blunt. If you tie a strip of fabric onto the handle of your fabric scissors, you'll remember which pair is which.

Thimble

A thimble is a tin or plastic finger protector; it keeps you from pricking your finger with the needle. Wear it on your middle finger. If you can't find one small enough, wrap adhesive tape or masking tape around your fingertip instead.

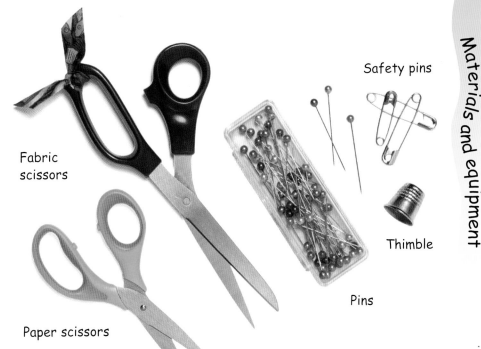

Fabric scissors

Paper scissors

Safety pins

Thimble

Pins

Fabrics

Most quilting is done on cotton fabric, as it's easy to handle and washes well. There are hundreds of fantastic fabrics made especially for patchwork and quilting and lots of stores that specialize in quilting fabrics.

When you buy fabric, it has a thin strip down both sides, which is woven tighter than the rest; this is called the selvage.

This side of the fabric is called the straight grain and won't pull out of shape if you give it a tug. The cross grain of the fabric will pull out of shape if you tug at it, so it's always best to use the straight grain of the fabric for the longest part of your project.

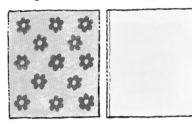

Right side   Wrong side

Selvage straight grain

Most fabrics have a right and a wrong side. It's usually easy to see which is which, because the pattern shows up more on the right side. Felt and fleece are very easy to use because they don't have a right or a wrong side, or a selvage, and they don't fray. How's that for an easy option! They also come in bright colors and patterns.

Patterned fabrics

Getting started

Batting

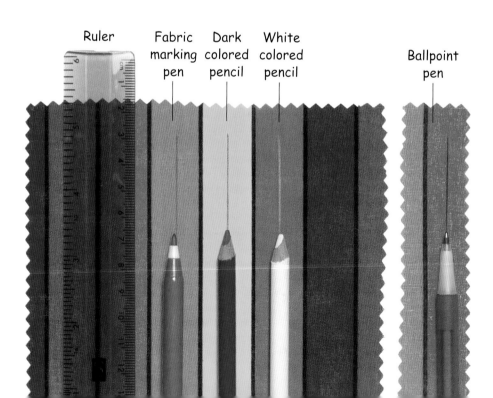

Threads

Batting

Batting is the fluffy fabric that goes in the middle of a quilt and gives it its warmth. It can be made from cotton or polyester. It comes by the yard (meter) and in different weights: lightweight 2-ounce (50-g) batting is fine for the projects in this book.

Threads

Ordinary sewing thread is fine for stitching pieces of fabric together. You can buy both cotton and polyester thread. Use cotton thread when you're sewing cotton fabric and polyester thread when sewing manmade fabrics.

There is also a special quilting thread, which is thicker and stronger than sewing thread. This is useful when you're stitching several layers of fabric together: you don't want your thread to break! However, you can strengthen ordinary sewing thread by pulling it across a cake of beeswax or a piece of candle. You can buy beeswax at quilt stores.

Thread comes in lots of different colors, but a mid-gray is a good color to choose, because it goes with both dark and light fabrics. If you want your thread to match your fabric, get a color that is slightly darker, as the stitches will blend in better.

Some of the projects in this book use pretty decorative stitches, and for this you will need thicker colored threads and six-strand embroidery floss. Embroidery floss comes in a bundle called a skein, which usually has both ends tied with a paper band. When you cut a length of thread, you can either use all six strands, which gives you a thick length of thread, or you can pull it in half so that you are using three strands. That way you get double the amount of thread from one skein!

Ruler

All you need is an ordinary ruler like the ones you use in school. You can also get big rulers made especially for quilting, but it's probably best to wait and see how much you enjoy quilting before you buy one.

Pencils, pens, and crayons

You will need to mark the fabric to show you where to stitch. To do this, you will need some colored pencils—a dark one for light fabrics and a white pencil for dark fabrics—or a special marking pen. Marking pens look like purple ink, but when they are wetted, the marks fade away. Take care not to mix these pens up with your ordinary felt-tip pens: if you use ordinary felt-tips, the marks won't come out.

To make light-colored marks, you can use slivers of soap instead of a white pencil. When the soap is nearly used up, dry it in a warm place, break a piece off, and use it in exactly the same way as a pencil to mark dark fabrics: it slides across the fabric nicely, rubs off when you have sewn the lines, and makes your hands smell nice!

You can also mark your work with a ballpoint pen. The ink tends to smudge, so use the pen on the wrong side of the fabric. Never use a pen on things that will need washing in case the color runs into the fabric.

Ruler   Fabric marking pen   Dark colored pencil   White colored pencil   Ballpoint pen

For some of the projects in this book, where you need to draw pictures or patterns on your fabric, you will need fabric crayons, which you can buy from craft stores. They look exactly like wax crayons, but when you iron them with a hot iron, the marks don't come off. Cover your drawing with some paper before you iron over it, so that the wax doesn't stick to the iron's hot plate. You will find full instructions for using fabric crayons on the packet.

Template cardboard or plastic

To make templates, you need either stiff cardboard, such as used greeting cards or cereal boxes, or special template plastic—sheets of see-through plastic, onto which you can trace templates straight from the book. If you are using cardboard, you will also need tracing paper, waxed paper used for cooking, or very thin paper, so that you can trace your pattern or shape onto the cardboard.

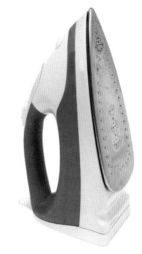

Iron

You need to iron your patchwork as you go. If you press each piece as soon as you have sewn it, the pieces will stay neat and keep their shape. Always press the iron onto the fabric rather than dragging it over the surface or the fabric may stretch out of shape. You can make a small ironing board out of a cardboard center from a bolt of fabric, which the fabric stores usually throw away. Cover it with some batting and then some cotton fabric, and you have your own handy-sized ironing board.

A small travel iron is very good, as it's smaller and lighter in weight than a normal iron. You might want to ask an adult to help you with any ironing. Always store a hot iron on its end, so that it doesn't burn the ironing board, and remember to switch it off after you have used it.

Fusible bonding web

Fusible bonding web has paper on one side and glue on the other. It's used to stick one fabric to another, and it's a great way of cutting out fancy shapes and sticking them to a background fabric without having to do any careful stitching. You have to iron it in place, so you might want to ask an adult to help with this.

Template plastic and card

Seam ripper

A seam ripper is a little tool that has a hook covering a sharp edge. When you run it along a machined seam, it will cut through the stitches so that you can undo the seam. Ideally, this won't be necessary, but it is a useful tool to have if you have made a mistake.

Fusible bonding web

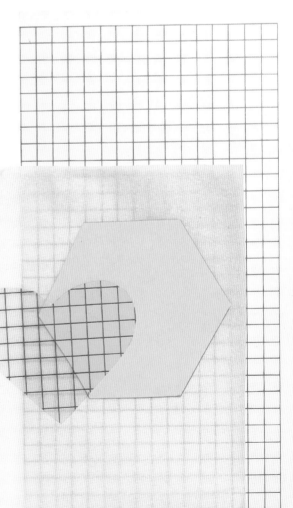

Getting started

Basic skills

There are some basic sewing skills that you will need to learn before you start to make the projects in this book. You may already know some of them, but in case you're a complete beginner, here are some tips to get you started.

Marking the fabric

The first thing you need to do is mark the fabric with lines that show you where to cut and where to sew. You can do this using a colored pencil or hard soap, a special marking pen, or even a ballpoint pen so long as you make the marks on the back of the fabric (see page 10).

Cutting fabric

When you've marked the fabric, you can cut along these lines to cut the piece to the size and shape that you want. Use fabric scissors to cut the fabric. Put the fabric on a table or a board, so that it's flat, as this makes it easier to cut. Make sure that you don't accidentally cut through any tablecloth underneath—or you'll be very unpopular!

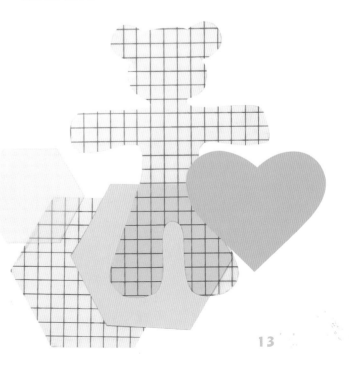

Cutting shapes

If you want to copy a special shape onto the fabric, you need to make something called a template. To do this, cut the shape you want out of either cardboard or plastic, place it on the fabric, and draw around it so that you copy the shape exactly.

When you've made your template, remember to write on it which project it is for. If you need several templates for a project, store them all together in an envelope so that you can find them easily next time you want to make the same thing.

CARDBOARD TEMPLATES

You can make templates from stiff cardboard: cereal boxes or old greeting cards are ideal.

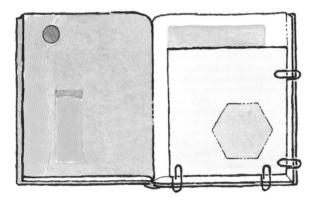

1 First, put a piece of tracing paper, waxed paper, or typing paper that is thin enough to see through over the pattern in the book and trace around it. To hold the paper down while you trace around the shape, attach the paper to the book with paper clips.

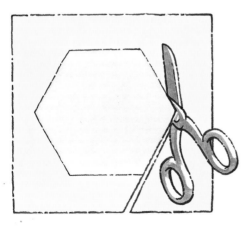

2 Using paper glue, stick the tracing to some cardboard, and then cut out the shape with paper scissors. Try to do this really neatly, so that you don't get any rough edges. You can keep the templates to use again.

PLASTIC TEMPLATES

Plastic templates are made from a thick plastic sheet, known as template plastic, which you buy from craft stores.

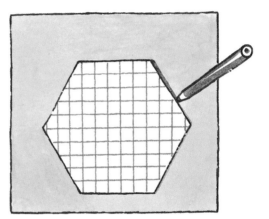

Trace the shape as before, but this time trace it directly onto the plastic. Cut out the shape with paper scissors. You can then draw around the template, directly onto the fabric.

13

Getting started

Threading a needle

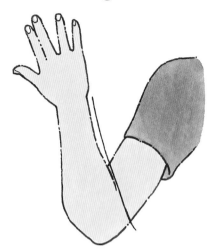

1 Pull the thread from the bobbin, making sure it is no longer than the distance between your elbow and your wrist. It might seem easier to have a really long piece of thread, so you don't have to keep threading your needle, but a long thread tends to knot and tangle. There's an old saying, "Long braid, lazy maid."

2 Cut the end of the thread at an angle to make it easier to thread through the eye of the needle. Some people lick the thread end. Pull about three-quarters of the thread through the needle eye and make a knot on the end of the longer thread, so that you can't pull the thread out of the fabric by mistake.

Making a knot

1 Wind the thread once around your forefinger about ½ inch (1.25 cm) from the tip and hold it in place with your thumb. Rub your thumb over your finger until the thread forms a knot.

2 You can pull half of the thread through the eye of the needle, knot both ends together, and use the thread double. The advantage of this is that the needle won't slip off the thread if you pull too hard. The disadvantage is that if you make a mistake, it's difficult to unpick the threads, whereas if you have used a single thread, you can take your needle off, pull out the stitches, and thread the needle again.

Tip

Another way of securing your stitches when you begin to sew is to start with a backstitch (see next page).

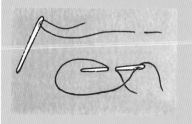

Finishing off your stitches

This is important, because you don't want all your hard work to unravel.

One way of finishing off is to make a backstitch (see next page)—or, to be really secure, two backstitches.

You can also knot the thread and cut off the end. To do this, make a small backstitch—but instead of pulling the thread all the way through, leave a loop. Then take the needle through this loop and pull the thread until a second loop forms; take the needle back through the second loop, pull tight, and cut off the thread.

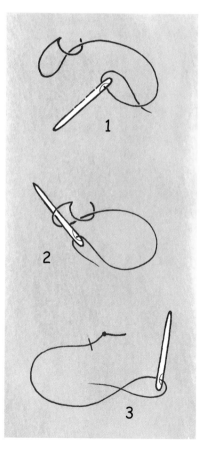

To learn how to finish off when doing a quilting stitch, see Quilting Techniques, page 41.

Basic stitches

There are lots of different stitches that you can use in quilting. Some are used to join pieces of fabric together, and others are just for decoration. Here are some of the most common.

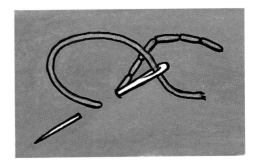

Backstitch Backstitch is used to start and end a row of stitches. You can also make a seam of running stitch stronger by adding a backstitch every six stitches or so. Bring the needle from the back to the front of the fabric, then push the needle back down through the fabric about ⅛ inch (0.3 cm) behind the point where it first came up. Bring the needle up again ⅛ inch (0.3 cm) ahead of the thread and pull the stitch tight.

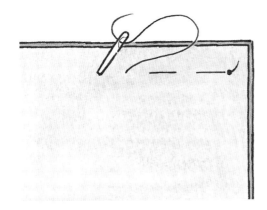

Basting stitch This is a large, straight stitch that is used to hold pieces of fabric together, or to hold a hem flat, before you machine- or hand-stitch. To make the first stitch, push the needle all the way through the fabric from the top, bring it back up about ½ inch (1.25 cm) away from where you first pushed it in, and pull the thread tight, taking care not to pucker the fabric. Push the needle back down into the fabric ½ inch (1.25 cm) from where the thread is. Repeat, taking ½ inch (1.25 cm) stitches, and finish with a knot.

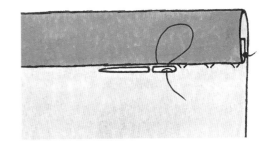

Hem stitch Hem stitch, which is also called slip stitch, is used to make hems where the edge of the fabric is turned under. Fasten the thread to the folded edge of the fabric with a knot. Working from right to left, pick up a single thread of the fabric just below the folded edge. Put the needle into the fold above and bring it out ¼ inch (0.6 cm) away. Pick up another thread in the fabric below the point where the needle came out and continue like this, taking one stitch in the fold and one in the fabric.

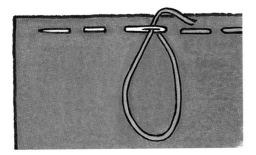

Running stitch Running stitch is used to join pieces of fabric together. Start by making a knot or a backstitch, and then weave the needle in and out of the fabric several times before pulling the needle through the fabric. The stitches and the spaces between them should be the same length—about ⅛ inch (0.3 cm).

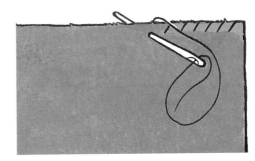

Oversewing (whipstitching) This stitch covers the raw edges of the fabric and holds them together. Make a knot in the thread and bring the needle from the back to the front of the fabric ¼ inch (0.6 cm) from the raw edge. Bring the thread over the top of the fabric and bring the needle back to the front ⅛ inch (0.3 cm) away from the first stitch.

Fancy embroidery stitches

Some of the projects use fancy embroidery stitches for decoration. You can use any stitches you like, which is a great way of making your projects look different from everyone else's. Some of these stitches are also a useful way of covering up raw edges and preventing them from fraying.

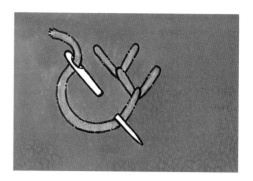

Feather stitch This is another looped decorative stitch. As with blanket stitch, you may find it's easiest to start by drawing a line to sew along. Make a knot in the thread and bring the needle through from the back of the fabric to the front a little to the right of the marked line. Holding the thread down with your thumb take a small diagonal stitch above the thread on the left of the line. Repeat on the opposite side of the line. Continue working on alternate sides of the line. You can vary the effect by taking two stitches on each side of the line.

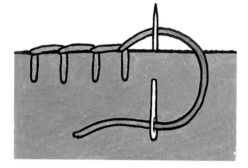

Blanket stitch Blanket stitch was originally used on blankets, which is how it gets its name. It is used to make a decorative border on fabric that won't fray, such as felt, and to cover raw edges.

You may find it easiest to start by drawing two parallel lines about ½ inch (1.25 cm) apart as guidelines to sew on. If you're using the stitch to cover an edge, draw a line ½ inch (1.25 cm) from the edge. Working from left to right, make a knot in the thread, bring the needle through from the back of the fabric to the front on the lower line, and put the needle into the top line a little to the right. Take a stitch, bringing it out on the bottom line directly below, keeping the thread under the point of the needle, and pull it through to make a looped stitch.

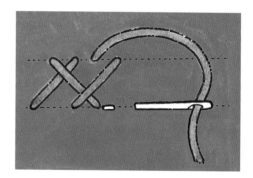

Herringbone stitch This stitch is used both for decoration and for securing hems on thick fabric. Draw two lines about ½ inch (1.25 cm) apart. Working from left to right, make a knot in the thread and bring the needle through from the back to the front on the bottom line. Take the needle up to the top line ½ inch (1.25 cm) away from the first stitch on the right, and take a small stitch to the left on the top line. Put the needle back in on the bottom line about ½ inch (1.25 cm) to the right of the first stitch, and take a stitch to the left. The thread crosses back up to the top line.

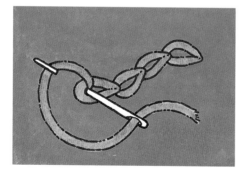

Chain stitch This is a looped stitch and can be used in straight lines or curved. Make a knot in the thread. Working from right to left, bring the needle through from the back of the fabric to the front. Loop the thread under the needle, put the needle back where the thread came out, and take a small stitch.

Using pins

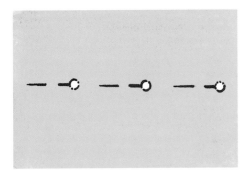

Always have straight pins pointing in the same direction, so that you don't prick your finger while you're sewing.

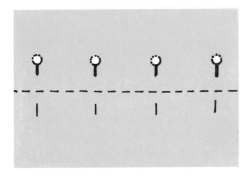

If you are using a sewing machine, put your pins in at right angles to the edge of the fabric, so that you can pull them out as you sew or sew over them without breaking the needle.

Store both straight and safety pins in a tin or box away from small brothers or sisters.

Getting started

Using a sewing machine

Some of the projects in this book involve using a sewing machine, but if you don't have one, don't worry: you can also do these projects by hand; it will just take a little longer!

- Always ask an adult's permission if you are borrowing the machine, and always return the stitch to the one that the machine was set at when you started.
- Sit directly across from the needle. You might need a cushion on your chair so you are at a comfortable height.

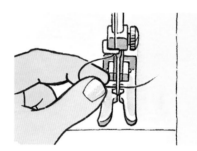

- Ask for help with threading the machine and the bobbin, as the bobbin is slightly different in each make of machine. There is usually a good instruction book with a machine, so look at the diagrams in it before you start.

Straight stitching

To make it easier to keep on the line, sew along the line you've drawn in pencil ¼ inch (0.6 cm) from the edge of the fabric. When you get more experienced, you can use the edge of the machine foot to guide you.

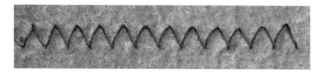

Zigzag stitch

Most machines have this stitch. It's very useful for joining two raw edges together before you bind the edges.

- Try the stitches out first on a spare scrap of fabric—and always keep your fingers well away from the needle when you're using a sewing machine.

Fancy embroidery stitches

If your machine has these, they are a lot of fun to use. Try them out in different-colored threads and sizes.

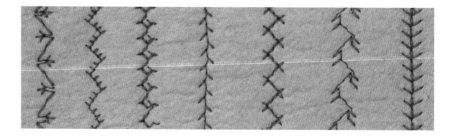

Binding the edges

Binding is a way of covering raw edges with fabric. It keeps them from fraying and can make a seam strong, which is great for projects such as bags and purses.

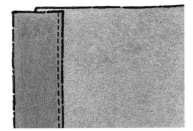

1 We are using bias binding on some of the projects; this is a strip of fabric that you buy by the yard (meter) and has the edges turned under. Pin the binding to one of the raw edges about ¼ inch (0.6 cm) from the edge. Hem- or straight-stitch along the edge, removing the pins as you go.

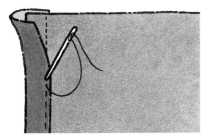

2 Now fold the binding to the other side so that it covers the raw edge, pin it down, and hem it in place. When you get near the end, turn under a small seam of about ¼ inch (0.6 cm) and hem down to make it look nice and neat. If it looks a bit messy, you can always cover up the evidence with a button!

Now that you have got the basic skills, you're ready to start making all the fun projects in the book. You'll also learn some extra things as you go along. Welcome to the world of quilting!

Sewing on buttons

In some of the projects, we use buttons for decoration—as the eyes on butterflies and the centers of flowers. We also use buttons to attach loops to the top of a quilt. Being able to sew on buttons is really useful—maybe you could increase your pocket money by offering to sew your family's lost buttons onto their shirts!

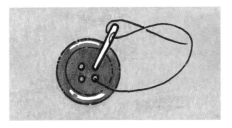

1 Use double thread to sew on a button, as it will be stronger and the button won't come off. Make a knot in the thread and bring the needle up from the back of the fabric, bringing the needle through the hole of the button. Some buttons have two holes and some have four. Put the needle back into the back of the fabric through the next hole of the button. Do this four or five times.

2 Now bring the needle through to the front of the fabric under the holes of the button and wrap the thread around the base of the button four or five times.

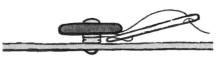

3 Make a knot through a loop and cut off the thread. This makes a very strong fastening. If the button has four holes, you can sew the thread in either a crisscross pattern or in two lines.

Simple piecing techniques

Simple piecing can be done by hand, or by machine. Both methods will become easier with practice.

Pinning and basting

The first thing you need to do is pin and baste the fabrics together. This gives you the chance of being sure that the pieces join up before you start doing the final stitching. It also keeps the pieces from slipping out of position while you're sewing. Pinning and basting takes a lot of time, but it makes things easier in the long run. People who have done a lot of sewing sometimes leave out this stage.

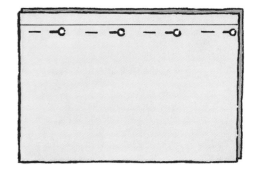

2 Place the two pieces of fabric right sides together, so that you're looking at the wrong side. Pin the fabrics together below the line that you drew, making sure that all the pins are facing the same way. Check the edges to make sure that the pieces fit exactly on top of each other.

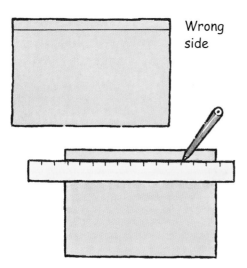

Wrong side

1 On the wrong side of the fabric (the side without the pattern), draw a line along your ruler ¼ inch (0.6 cm) from the edge to be sewn. This gives you a guide to follow when you're stitching. If your fabric is light colored, use a pencil; if the fabric is dark, use a light-colored pencil or a piece of hard soap.

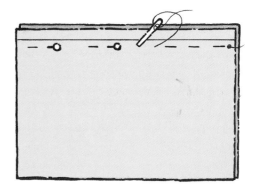

3 Thread a needle and make a knot in the end of the thread. Put a thimble on your third finger and baste the two pieces together (see page 15). Take out the pins as you go.

Sewing the pieces together

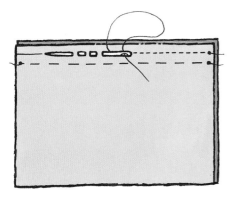

Now everything's ready for you to sew the pieces together permanently.

Thread a needle and make a knot in the end of the thread. Put a thimble on your third finger and sew along the line that you drew at the very beginning, using a running stitch (see page 15). With practice, you will be able to make small stitches and to put more stitches on your needle at a time. When you've finished the final stitching, take out the basting stitches.

Machine piecing

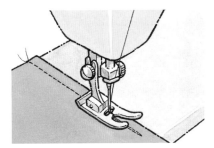

First of all, make sure your chair is at the right height: you might need to put an extra cushion on the chair. You should be able to reach the machine without having to stretch, as it could make your back sore if you sew for any length of time. Some quilters use chairs like the ones used in offices, which can be made higher or lower. Any chair that has a straight back and no arms is suitable.

If you are stitching fabrics together by machine, mark, pin, and baste just as you would if you were stitching by hand. The actual sewing won't take you as long. Concentrate hard and don't let the machine wobble off your drawn line. Otherwise you will have to unpick the stitches and start again. Some machines can be set to sew at half the normal speed, which makes it easier to keep the lines straight. If your machine doesn't do this, try not to put your foot down hard. It's like driving a car: the harder you put your foot down, the faster it goes. Practice on some paper or scraps of waste fabric to start with and you'll soon get the hang of it.

When you start and end a seam on the machine, do a few stitches forward and then a few stitches backward, so that the stitches won't unravel.

Always remember to switch off the sewing machine when you've finished sewing.

Pressing

When you've joined both pieces together, you should press the seams with your fingers or iron them to make the fabric lie flat. "Pressing" means exactly what it says: you should press the iron down on the seam, not drag it over the fabric. Otherwise the fabric may stretch.

Irons can get very hot, so you might want to get an adult to help you with this. Irons have different heat settings, so make sure you set it to the right temperature for the fabric you're using, as some fabrics might melt. This not only spoils your hard work, but also makes a nasty mess on the iron.

If you're joining a light-colored fabric to a dark one, press the seam toward the dark fabric; then it won't show through on the light fabric. It's best to press the seam one way, rather than open it out flat, as this makes the seam stronger.

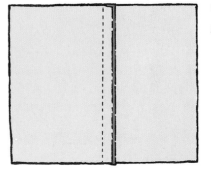

Wrong side

Dandy dinosaur bag

Hang this bag at the end of your bed or on a hook on the wall, and use it to keep your special treasures safe. If dinosaurs aren't your thing, decorate your bag with something else, such as flowers, butterflies, or flying saucers. It's your bag, so you decide. Simply cut out your shapes so that they are around the same size as the dinosaur templates on the opposite page.

Simple piecing

Materials

- Muslin that has been washed and dried
- - - - - - - - - - - - - - - - - -
- Assortment of brightly colored, patterned fabrics
- - - - - - - - - - - - - - - - - -
- Paper and fabric scissors
- - - - - - - - - - - - - - - - - -
- Fabric crayons
- - - - - - - - - - - - - - - - - -
- Thin ribbon or tape 45 inches (114 cm) long
- - - - - - - - - - - - - - - - - -
- Needle and thread
- - - - - - - - - - - - - - - - - -
- Pins
- - - - - - - - - - - - - - - - - -
- Safety pin
- - - - - - - - - - - - - - - - - -
- Ruler

How to make the dinosaur bag

1 Cut six pieces of plain muslin, all 10 x 8 inches (25 x 20 cm).

2 Cut six pieces of patterned fabric, all 10 x 8 inches (25 x 20 cm). These can have different patterns, or be the same pattern.

▲ Hold the template on the fabric and draw around it carefully.

3 Draw a dinosaur (or your chosen shape) in pencil or pen on each plain piece of muslin. If you find this difficult, trace one of the dinosaurs on the opposite page, cut it out, and stick it onto cardboard, such as an old cereal box. Cut out the cardboard with paper scissors to make a template. You can now draw around this onto your fabric.

Templates
shown at 70% size
enlarge to 140%

4 Color in your dinosaurs with fabric crayons. When you've finished, cover each one with paper and press with an iron. (Ask an adult to help with this.) This makes sure that the picture will not come off when the fabric is washed.

▲ Number the patches 1 to 6 on the wrong side (back) of your fabric.

5 Arrange the pieces on a table or the floor, 2 patches (or blocks) wide and 3 patches long. Make sure you have a dinosaur patch next to a patterned patch, as shown in the drawing.

▶ A great-looking bag to fill with treasures or sneakers.

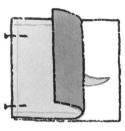

▲ Draw a line ¼ inch (0.6 cm) from the edge on the wrong side of the fabric.

6 On the wrong side of the 6 blocks, draw a line all around, ¼ inch (0.6 cm) from the edge, using pencil, pen, marking pencil, or soap. This is the line you will sew along. Number the blocks on the back, so you know which ones to sew together. Do this on the very edge of the fabric, so it won't show when you have finished sewing.

▲ Sew along the line you have drawn on the wrong side of the fabric.

7 Join patches 1 and 2 along the shortest edge and pin them together, making sure that your dinosaur is not upside down. Either sew along the line with a sewing machine, or hand-sew it with a running stitch (see page 15). Remember to sew along the line on the wrong side of the fabric.

▲ Check that the dinosaurs are the right way up before sewing the blocks together.

8 Now sew block 3 to block 4, and block 5 to block 6.

9 Iron your patches flat along the seams, or press the joins hard with your fingers to flatten them.

10 Place the patches on the table or floor and make sure they are in the right place, looking at the drawing again to check.

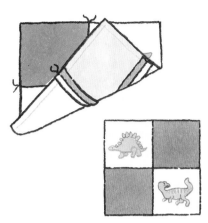

⚠ When sewing four blocks together, try to make the joins meet in the middle.

⚠ Arrange your patches in a checkered effect, where each patterned block is next to a dinosaur block.

11 Pin and sew blocks 1 and 2 to blocks 3 and 4, so block 1 will be sewn above block 3, and block 2 will be above block 4. Don't panic if the seams don't join up perfectly—it can take a lot of practice to get joins neat, and your bag will still look great even if your joins are slightly lopsided.

12 Join blocks 5 and 6 to blocks 3 and 4, to finish one side of your bag.

13 Repeat steps 5 to 12 with the remaining six fabric patches. You will find it gets easier with every block you join.

14 Join the two pieces of your bag together, so blocks 2, 4, and 6 on one piece of the bag are next to blocks 1, 3, and 5 on the other piece of the bag. Remember to sew along the lines on the wrong side of the fabric and check that none of the dinosaurs are upside down before you start to sew.

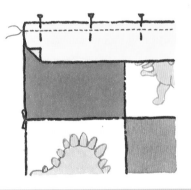

⚠ Sew the right sides of the fabric together, with the strip's wrong side facing outward.

15 Cut a length of patterned fabric 38 inches (97 cm) long and 3 inches (8 cm) wide. Sew this along the top of the bag, across four blocks, as shown in the drawing.

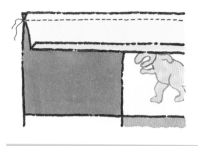

▲ Ask an adult to help if you press the seams with an iron.

16 Press the seam. Then fold in the opposite rough edge by about ¼–½ inch (0.6–1.25 cm).

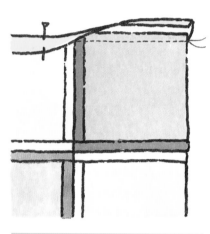

▲ Fold the strip over on the wrong side of the fabric. Sew the strip down firmly so the bag will be strong.

17 Fold this piece of fabric over the raw edge of the bag, pin it down, and sew along the edge. This makes a channel for the ribbon, so you can draw the top of the bag together.

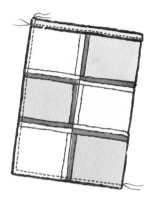

▲ Complete the bag by sewing up the final two edges. Make sure the wrong sides are facing out.

18 Fold the bag in half so that the right sides of the fabric are facing each other, and sew along the remaining two raw edges to finish your bag.

▲ Using a safety pin makes it easy to push the ribbon through the channel.

19 Cut some thin ribbon or tape 45 inches (114 cm) long and attach one end to a safety pin.

▲ Make sure that the holes go through only one layer of fabric.

20 Make two small holes with some scissors on each side of the seam in your channel. Make sure the holes are on the wrong side of the fabric, and push the scissors through only one layer of fabric. Ask an adult to help with this. Thread the safety pin and ribbon through the hole and push it through the channel. When you have pushed it through to the other end, take off the pin and tie the ribbon in a knot.

21 Turn the fabric right side out, pull the ribbon, and fill your dandy dinosaur bag with sneakers, treasures, or treats.

Tip

When pressing the seams, always press to the dark side of the fabric so the seam doesn't show through on the light side.

For the plain squares, really bright fabric works very well. Stores often sell scraps at good prices.

English pieced hexagon mat

This kind of piecing is a very old method of patchwork used before sewing machines were available to most families. In fact, if you asked your grandmother what kind of patchwork she did first, she would probably say "hexagons." Hexagon piecing is fun to do because it's small to work with, so you can take a bag of patches with you on a long trip. It is also very easy once you get the hang of it. A hexagon is a geometric shape with six sides. You can also use other geometric shapes in patchwork, such as octagons, which have eight sides. Depending on the type of fabric you have, you can use this pattern to make a mat, a Christmas decoration, a Christmas wreath, or a pincushion—all great for presents! The shape of this mat looks like a flower. A long time ago, women made whole bed-sized quilts like this, and the pattern is called "Grandmother's Garden."

Materials

- Thick paper or thin cardboard
- Template plastic (optional)
- Sharp pencil
- Paper scissors
- An assortment of fabric scraps
- Fabric scissors
- Needle
- Sewing thread
- Glue stick

How to make the hexagon mat

1 Make a hexagon template by tracing around template 1. Stick your tracing onto a piece of cardboard (old greeting cards are perfect for this), and cut it out carefully. If the sides of your template are wobbly, your fabric hexagon pieces will not fit together, so it is worth taking care with this stage.

If you are using template plastic, place it over this book, trace the hexagon onto the plastic, then cut it out. If you are good at math, you can make your own hexagons. Read the instructions in the box to find out how.

How to Make a Hexagon Template

WHAT YOU NEED
- Compasses
- Sharp pencil
- Ruler
- Cardboard

1 Decide how big the hexagon is going to be (that is, the length of the sides).

2 Set the compasses to this measurement.

3 Draw a circle this size on the cardboard.

4 Keeping the compasses set at the same size, put the point anywhere on the circumference (the outer edge of the circle). For example, put the compass point at point a, and draw an arc so that it crosses the circumference at point b. Now put the compass point at b and draw another arc at c. Keep going until you have made six arcs. The last one should cross the circle at a.

5 Connect points a-b-c-d-e-f with a ruler to form the sides of the hexagon.

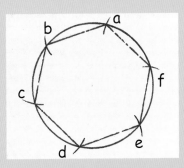

Make the points of the hexagon with the compasses, then connect the lines to form the hexagon's straight edges.

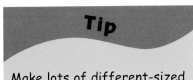

▲ Cut around the hexagons with paper scissors, keeping the edges sharp and neat.

2 Draw around your template 14 times on thick paper or thin cardboard. Try to be as neat as possible and make the corners sharp. Cut out the templates with paper scissors.

Tip

Make lots of different-sized hexagons to practice.

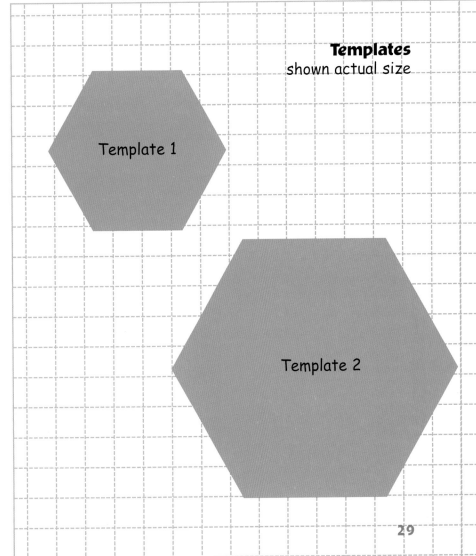

Templates
shown actual size

Template 1

Template 2

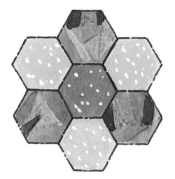

▲ Hexagon mat made out of three different fabrics.

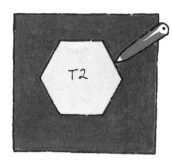

▲ Draw around template 2 onto your fabric. Write a large "2" on it, so you know which template is which.

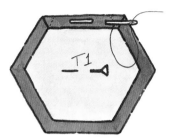

▲ Fold over the edge of the fabric and baste to the paper.

▲ Hexagon mat made out of seven different fabrics.

4 Trace template 2 and stick onto cardboard, to make a hexagon ¼ inch (0.6 cm) larger than the other template. Draw around this template onto your fabric and cut out 14 hexagon pieces.

▲ Fold over the corners, one at a time, and sew around the hexagon shape.

3 Now you can choose your fabrics. If you are making a Christmas mat or decoration, choose a fabric with a Christmas pattern, or something with sparkly gold threads. You need enough fabric to make 14 patches (seven on each side). It often looks best to have the center patch a different color from the patches around the outside. For the outer hexagons, you can either have three patches made out of one kind of patterned fabric and three patches made out of another patterned fabric, or you can make each patch a different color and pattern.

▲ Cut out the fabric ¹⁄₄ inch (0.6 cm) larger than each paper hexagon.

5 Alternatively, you can pin your paper hexagons to the wrong side of the fabric and cut them out, leaving ¼ inch (0.6 cm) of fabric around the outside. Use whichever method you find easiest. This method is often best for sparkly fabrics, which are difficult to draw on.

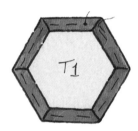

▲ Finish off with a backstitch to secure the thread.

6 Baste the fabric to the paper hexagon by turning the edge of the fabric over the paper. Make sure the fabric is tight and neat as you fold it over each corner. Baste all the way around and finish with a backstitch. Do the other 13 hexagons in the same way.

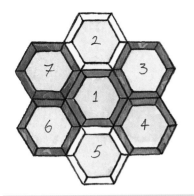

▲ Number your patches from 1 to 7, starting with the patch in the center.

7 Arrange your patches into groups of seven (seven for the front and seven for the back), switching them around until you are happy with the arrangement of colors and patterns. Number the patches on the paper, starting with the hexagon in the center.

▲ Join patches 1 and 2 together by whipstitching the edges.

8 Sew patches 1 and 2 together, making sure the patches are exactly on top of each other, right sides facing. Carefully whipstitch the edges, using small, neat stitches. Try not to sew through the cardboard or paper, so that you can reuse the templates. Finish off with two or three stitches sewn over each other to secure the thread. Open out the two patches.

9 Now sew patch 3 to patch 2, again with right sides facing together.

10 Next, sew patch 3 to patch 1.

11 Continue in the same way until all seven patches are sewn together. Then sew your other seven patches together to make the back of the mat.

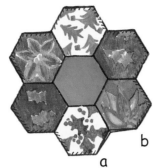

▲ Sew both sides of the mat together, leaving a gap (a–b).

12 Put both sides of your mat together, right sides outside, match up the corners, and pin the pieces to keep them together. Neatly whipstitch the outer edges of the hexagons, leaving a small gap, as shown in the drawing.

13 Cut the basting threads, pull out the threads, and remove the paper so that you can reuse it.

▲ To make a Christmas tree decoration, add a loop.

14 If you want to make a mat, sew up the gap, from a to b. For a pincushion, fill it with some stuffing before whipstitching. Make a Christmas decoration in the same way as a pincushion, but stitch in a hanging loop in gold ribbon as you sew up the gap.

Tips

● You can sew the two sides of the mat together with the right sides of the fabric facing, then turn it the right way around for the final bit of sewing from a to b. It is a good idea to do this if your whipstitching is not very neat.

● If you want to make a pincushion, choose flowery fabrics—it's a great way to use up scraps.

Seashore scenes quilt

This little quilt will show you how to piece triangles to make squares, then make the squares into a picture of a boat. It is tie quilted, which is a traditional way of quilting three layers of fabric together. It gives the quilt a puffy look, and the ties of thread look like strands of seaweed in the sea and flags on the boat.

How to make the seashore scenes quilt

1 Using a sharp pencil and ruler, draw four squares measuring 4 inches (10 cm), and two squares measuring 4½ inches (11 cm) on the blue fabric for the sky.

▲ Cut six squares out of the sky blue fabric. If possible, find a fabric printed with fluffy white clouds.

Materials

- Blue fabric for sky—four 4 inch (10 cm) squares, and two 4½ inch (11 cm) squares
- White fabric for sails—two 4½ inch (11 cm) squares
- Red fabric for boat—two 4 inch (10 cm) squares, one 4½ inch (11 cm) square
- Dark blue fabric for sea—one 4½ inch (11 cm) square, and a large piece 14 x 8 inches (35 x 20 cm)
- Sharp pencil
- Ruler
- Scissors
- Needle

- Thread
- Sewing machine (optional)
- Fabric with fish, shells, mermaids
- Bonding web
- Iron
- Batting 14 x 18 inches (35 x 46 cm)
- Backing fabric in a dark color 17 x 21 inches (43 x 53 cm)
- Safety pins
- Thick thread in red and green (this can be embroidery floss)

▲ Cut the squares diagonally to make two triangles.

2 Cut out the squares with scissors. Draw a diagonal line across each of the two bigger squares and cut across the line to make four triangles.

Simple piecing

Tip

See if you can find some blue fabric with clouds already printed on it to make a fantastic sky.

3 Draw two 4½-inch (11-cm) squares on the white fabric and repeat step 2 to make four white triangles.

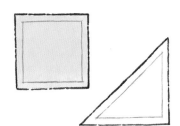

△ Draw sewing guidelines around every piece, ¼ inch (0.6 cm) from the edge.

4 Using a ruler, draw a pencil line on the wrong side of the fabric on all the squares and triangles, ¼ inch (0.6 cm) from the edge. Use this line to guide you when you sew the pieces together.

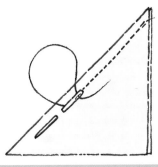

△ Sew the blue and white triangles together along the diagonal line.

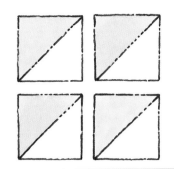

△ Join four blue to four white triangles, to make four new squares.

5 Join one blue triangle and one white triangle together, sewing along the diagonal line. Press open the seams with an iron, flattening the light side of the fabric over the dark side so that it will not show through when you turn the fabric the right way around.

Tips

● To keep your fabric from sliding when you're drawing lines on it, put the fabric on sandpaper to hold it in place.

● To help you get the pieces in the right place, simply lay your patches on the table as if you are doing a jigsaw puzzle and take up one piece at a time as you sew it. That way, you can see that it looks like a ship sailing against the sky.

● Turn to General Instructions, page 21, for help on pressing open seams.

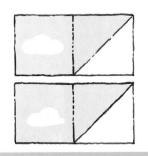

△ Join two blue-and-white squares to two blue squares.

6 Repeat this for the other triangles. Join two blue-and-white squares to two blue squares, making sure that the blue square is next to the blue side of the blue-and-white triangle.

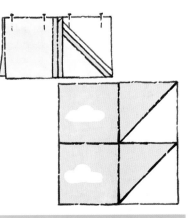

△ Place the fabric pieces with right sides facing, and secure with pins, pushed in vertically. Press open the joined seams with an iron.

7 Join together these two rectangles to make a square. Place the pieces with the right sides together and pin down the seam join in the middle. To make sure that it is really accurate, put the pins in vertically, so that they stick upward. This makes it easier to sew with the pins left in. If you are using a machine, you can sew over the pins without breaking the needle. Sew along the lines you have drawn in step 4, then press open the triangles to make a square, as you did in step 5.

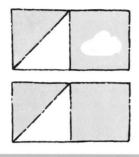

▲ Join the remaining triangles to the squares, with the white triangles next to the blue squares.

8 Join two of the squares to the remaining two triangle squares. This time, join the white triangle side to the blue square. Join them together as you did in step 7.

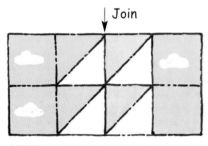

Join

▲ Sew together the squares so that the sails are pointing the same way.

9 Join your squares together so that the sails are pointing the right way, following the drawing above. Put in your pins so that you get a neat join, and make sure the plain blue squares are on the outside, not in the middle. Iron the squares, as before.

10 Draw and cut out the squares from the red fabric (to make the boat's hull), and the square from the sea fabric.

11 Draw a line diagonally across the sea fabric square and the larger red square, and cut across the line to make four triangles. Draw a line ¼ inch (0.6 cm) from the edge of the squares and triangles, as in step 5.

▲ Join two red squares together, and press the seams.

12 Sew the two red squares together along the line.

▲ Join the red triangles to the sea fabric triangles.

13 Sew the red triangles to the sea triangles, as shown in the drawing.

▲ Sew the red triangles to the red squares, to make a boat shape.

14 Sew the two squares you've just made to the red rectangle to form a boat shape.

15 Sew the boat shape to the sails, with right sides together and pins sticking upward at all the joins.

16 Sew your piece of sea fabric onto the bottom of the boat.

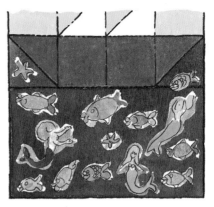

▲ Arrange some fussy cut shapes and bonded images on the square of sea fabric below the boat.

17 Find some fabric decorated with fish, starfish, mermaids, and shells. Iron bonding web onto the back of the bits you want to use and fussy cut around them (See page 56).

Tip

If you don't have any fancy fabric for the sea creatures, draw your own with fabric crayons, fussy cut around them, and bond them onto the pictures. If you like, add a treasure chest filled with gold coins.

18 Position your fish, mermaids, and shells onto the sea fabric. It is usually best to have an odd number of things—so three mermaids look better than two, or five fish look better than four. When you are happy with your arrangement, iron the pieces to bond them onto the sea fabric.

19 To make the quilt into a wall hanging, put the backing fabric on the table, then place the batting on top of the backing fabric, and your picture on top of the batting. Pin the pieces of fabric together to hold them in position.

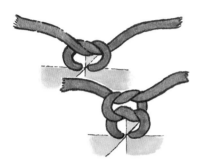

20 Thread a large-eyed needle with embroidery floss or thick colored thread. Push the needle in at the join of the sails, then come back through the fabric, making a small stitch so you have both threads on top of the work. Tie the threads with a reef knot, then cut the ends to about ½ inch (1.25 cm). Do this six times, through each of the sails.

21 The rest of the sea, which is a large area, can be tied in the same way but with green thread to look like seaweed. Make the knots between your fish and other pieces. It looks best if they are spaced randomly rather than being in a regular pattern.

▲ Fold over the edges of the backing fabric and hem them neatly all the way around the edge of the quilt.

22 For the finishing touches, fold over the backing and press it so it is about ¼ inch (0.6 cm) wide. Fold it over to the front and hem it with a thread the same color as the fabric, or quilt it with a contrast cotton thread.

Crazy patchwork bag

This bag is made in a kind of patchwork called **Crazy Patchwork**, in which odd-shaped scraps of fabric are sewn onto a larger piece of fabric. The raw edges are then covered either with fancy machine stitches or with embroidery stitches. Crazy patchwork probably started a long time ago, when people who did not have much money cut up their old, worn clothes and sewed the scraps into quilts to keep themselves warm. It was popular around 120 years ago, when ladies and young girls had plenty of time for sewing, and loved embroidering seams with clever stitches.

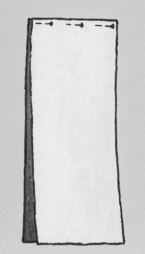

Simple piecing

Materials

● 7 x 20 inch (18 x 50 cm) fabric for the front of the bag
- - - - - - - - - - - - -
● 7 x 20 inch (18 x 50 cm) dark fabric for the lining
- - - - - - - - - - - - -
● Pins
- - - - - - - - - - - - -
● Selection of scraps of brightly colored fabrics
- - - - - - - - - - - - -
● Scissors
- - - - - - - - - - - - -
● Needle
- - - - - - - - - - - - -
● Embroidery flosses in bright colors (if sewing by hand) or a sewing machine that can do fancy stitches
- - - - - - - - - - - - -
● Bias binding (35 inches [89 cm])
- - - - - - - - - - - - -
● Ribbon for handle (25 inches [64 cm])
- - - - - - - - - - - - -
● Two buttons
- - - - - - - - - - - - -

How to make the crazy patchwork bag

▲ Pin the two pieces of fabric together, with the fabric for the front of the bag on top.

1 Place the fabric for the front of the bag on top of the lining fabric, and pin them together along the top edge.

Tip

Use a dark fabric for the rectangle that's underneath. This will be the inside of the bag, and if you use a dark color, dirty marks won't show! The other fabric can be any color, because it will all be covered up with the "crazy" scraps.

2 Cut your brightly colored fabric scraps into interesting shapes—squares, triangles, or any other shape that you like. If you're using fabrics that are printed with pictures, make sure you don't cut off important parts of the picture: teddy bears will look very strange without their heads, for example!

▲ Feather stitch over the edges of the fabric shapes to fix them firmly in place.

5 Now you can sew the patches in place by stitching around the edges of the fabric shapes. If you are using a sewing machine, find out if it can do fancy embroidery stitches. Read the instruction book before you start, and practice any new stitches on a scrap of fabric first; if the stitches have numbers, write the number on your practice piece, so that when you want to use that stitch again, it will be easy to find it. Some machines are computerized and have buttons to change the stitches.

▲ Pin fabric shapes all over the rectangle, until it is completely covered. It doesn't matter if they overlap each other a little.

▲ Any pictures on the top half of the rectangle have to be the right way up; those on the bottom half have to be upside down.

3 Place the shapes on the fabric rectangle and move them around to see where they look best. Try to balance out the colors, so that you don't get two pieces of the same color next to each other.

4 When you've made a pattern that you like, pin the fabric shapes in place. The bag is made by folding the rectangle in half, so if you have picture fabric of cars, teddy bears, or flowers, the pictures on the top half of the rectangle have to be the right way up, and the ones on the bottom half have to be upside down.

Fancy machine-embroidery stitches

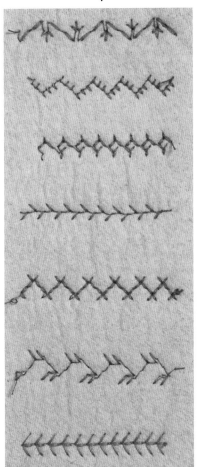

Tip

To make a really crazy bag, use scraps of fabric that are printed with pictures of animals, cars, fish, monsters, or anything else you can find.

Feather stitch

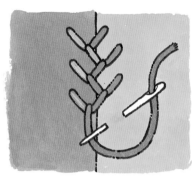

Blanket stitch

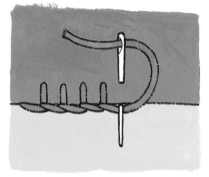

Herringbone stitch

▲ Try using two or three different stitches, in different colors, to make the bag look more interesting.

6 If you are working by hand, cover the raw edges with embroidery stitches. Cut a length of embroidery floss, which is made up of six strands of thread; hold three strands in one hand, and three in the other, and gently pull to divide the floss into two lengths. Feather stitch and herringbone stitch were often used in the old days, but you could also use blanket stitch.

7 When you've sewn on all the fabric shapes, turn the rectangle over, and press it with an iron so that it's flat. (Ask an adult to help you.) The reason for turning it over is that if you ironed it stitched side up, the stitches might get caught on the tip of the iron and get pulled out of shape.

▲ Bias binding keeps the edges of the bag from fraying.

8 Bind the top and bottom of the rectangle (the short sides) with bias binding; turn to page 19 to see how to do this.

▲ Fold the rectangle in half, so that you have stitched fabric shapes on both sides.

9 Fold the rectangle in half lengthwise, with the stitched shapes on the outside.

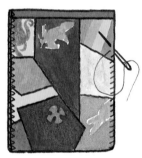

▲ Zigzag stitch (on the machine) or whipstitching (by hand) closes up the sides of the bag.

10 Sew the sides together. You can either use the zigzag stitch on the machine or, if you are working by hand, whipstitch the sides.

11 Bind the sides with bias binding, to cover the raw edges, as in step 8.

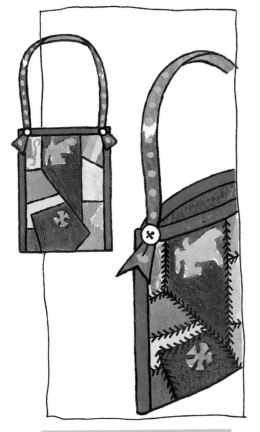

▲ A button at the base of each handle looks pretty.

12 To make the handle, either sew on a length of ribbon, or braid three strips of fabric together, and stitch one end of the ribbon or braid to each side of the bag. Cover the join where the handle meets the bag with a button; it looks pretty and hides any bad sewing.

Quilting techniques

Quilting means joining three layers of fabric—a front, a middle, and a back—together with small stitches. The middle layer is usually a fluffy fabric, and so quilted things are usually warm. Quilting is a great way of giving patchwork projects more texture and making them look good.

In the olden days, houses could be very cold in the winter. People made quilts for their beds to keep warm in the cold nights. Quilting was a very sociable thing to do. Women would get together to quilt all the patchwork tops that they'd made during the year. It was a great excuse for a party! These occasions were called quilting bees.

You will need

● A quilting needle (these are shorter and thinner than normal sewing needles)

● Thread (you can use quilting thread, which is stronger than sewing thread, but ordinary sewing thread will do)

● Thimble, and either a second thimble or adhesive tape

Making a "sandwich"

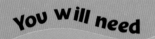

First you need to make a "sandwich" by putting the three layers of the quilt on top of one another. Put the backing right side down, with the batting on top and the quilt top right side up on top of the batting.

Make sure the front and back of the quilt are nice and smooth; iron them if necessary (or ask an adult to help you).

To hold the layers together, either pin them with safety pins or baste with large stitches, starting in the middle and working toward the edge; this keeps both the front and the back nice and smooth and free from tucks.

Marking quilting lines

The next thing you need to do is draw lines on your fabric to show you where to stitch. These lines should be visible, but not so dark that they show through the stitches. When marking, don't press too hard. It's a good idea to mark the quilting line in a color that matches the color of the thread you're using. You can also buy marking pens: when you wet the fabric, the pen marks fade away. Don't use an ordinary felt-tip, however, as the line won't ever come out.

For straight lines of quilting, you can stick strips of masking tape onto your quilt and quilt along the top and bottom edges. This is quicker than drawing lines.

You can also follow lines that you stitched on the quilt top when you pieced all the pieces of fabric together. If the quilting line follows the line of a seam or the edge of a patched shape, this is known as "quilting in the ditch."

How to quilt

Now you can start to quilt. Quilting is done with a stitch that you learned on page 15—a kind of running stitch. The stitches can be seen on the top of the work and you want it to look nice and neat, so try to make all your stitches the same length. Some people will be able to do tiny stitches and others somewhat larger stitches. It really doesn't matter what size they are, as long as you try to make them all the same. Girls used to be taught to do five stitches per inch (2.5 cm) of work. Get out your ruler and see how many you can do!

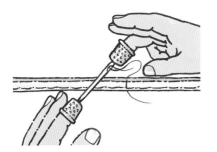

1 Put a thimble on the third finger of your stitching hand. You will be feeling for the needle under your work, so either wear another thimble on the first finger of your other hand or wind some masking tape or adhesive tape around this finger, so that you don't prick yourself.

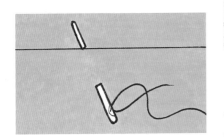

2 Thread a quilting needle and make a knot in the longer end of your thread. Now put the needle into the fabric on the right side about 1 inch (2.5 cm) away from where you want to start quilting. Bring the needle up at the point where you want to start stitching and pull gently: the knot will pop down under the top fabric and be hidden from view in the batting. This is so that the front and the back always look neat and the knots don't show.

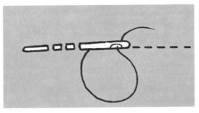

3 Sew with small, even running stitches, making sure you go through all three layers, and taking several stitches on the needle at a time. You will feel the needle come through to the finger that's underneath the fabric. It all seems strange at first, but after a little while, you will feel as if you've been quilting forever!

4 To finish off, you need to hide the knot. Make a knot like we did in basic techniques on page 14, but insert the needle back into the last stitch, making sure the knot is pulled down into the batting, and then pull the needle back through the top layer of the work about an inch from the last stitch and cut off the thread.

Contour quilting

As a variation, you can stitch a second (or even a third or fourth) line of quilting, following the shape of the first line. This is known as "contour quilting," because it looks like the contour lines on maps, which tell you how high hills and mountains are (see page 49). With practice, you will be able to judge where the lines should go, but to start with, it's a good idea to draw the line.

Big-stitch quilting

Big-stitch quilting is exactly what it says it is: it's the same as the quilting you've just learned to do, but you make bigger stitches. Big-stitch quilting is usually done in a bright color of thread, using thicker thread and a larger needle than normal. Big-stitch quilting is also called kantha quilting; it's used in Bangladesh, where they use it to embroider bright and colorful patterns, often of elephants. They use three layers of cotton fabric and no batting; it's so hot there that they don't need the extra warmth of the batting!

Quilt frames

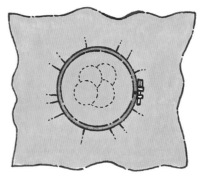

If you're quilting something very big, like a bed quilt, you can put the fabric on a frame to hold it in place while you work. Quilting frames can be very big—some of them are big enough for several people to use at the same time, and this is what people used in the olden days at quilting bees.

The quilting in this book is done without using a frame; it is called "lap quilting," because you quilt with the fabric on your lap.

Quilted pencil case

It's always nice to have a pencil case that looks different from everyone else's, and this case will be the envy of all your classmates. If you've never done any hand quilting before, this is a great project to start with: all you have to do is draw some straight lines on the fabric and stitch over them. To make things even easier, you could use striped fabric and stitch along the stripes.

How to make the quilted pencil case

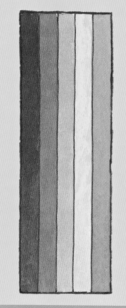

⚠ Mark lines on the fabric to show you where to stitch.

Materials

- Ruler
- Pencil, hard soap, or white crayon
- 17 x 4 inches (43 x 10 cm) fabric for the front of the pencil case
- 17 x 4 inches (43 x 10 cm) dark-colored fabric for the lining
- 17 x 4 inches (43 x 10 cm) batting

- Thimble
- Small needle
- Quilting or sewing thread in bright colors
- 30 inches (76 cm) bias binding
- 1 inch (2.5 cm) piece of Velcro or a snap

1 Using a ruler and a pencil (or a white crayon or a piece of hard soap, if you're using dark-colored fabric), draw faint lines ½ inch (1.25 cm) apart on the fabric for the front of the pencil case. For this one, we used striped fabric, so we just followed the lines of the stripes.

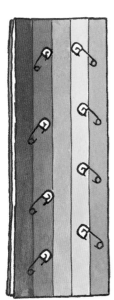

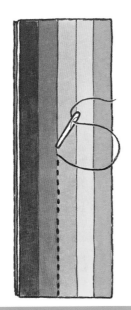

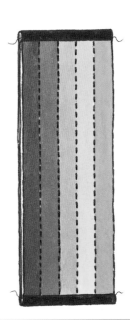

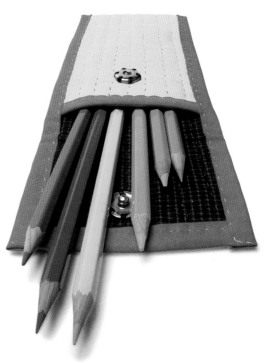

▲ Make a "sandwich" of your three fabrics, with the batting in the middle, and pin them together with safety pins.

▲ Start stitching in the middle and work outward.

▲ Bias binding looks neat—and it keeps the edges from fraying.

2 Place the lining fabric right side down on the table, with the batting on top of it, and the fabric for the front of the pencil case on top of the batting. (Make sure that the side on which you marked the lines in step 1 faces upward.) Pin the three layers together with safety pins, so that you won't prick your fingers.

3 Thread a small needle with brightly colored thread. Put a thimble on your middle finger. Stitch along the middle line that you drew in step 1, trying to keep all the stitches the same length.

4 If you've pulled the thread too tight, the fabric will look creased and puckered, but don't worry: put your thumb on one side of the fabric and your middle finger on the other, and gently run them along the stitched line to ease out the thread. Now do another line of quilting in a different color.

5 Continue until you have quilted all the lines.

6 Bind the top and bottom edges with bias binding. (Turn to page 19 to see how to do this.)

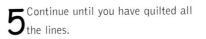

Tip

Use a dark-colored fabric for the lining, in case your felt-tip or ballpoint pens leak onto it.

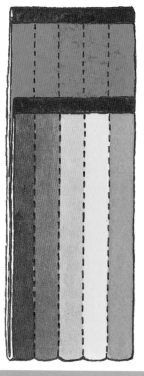

⚠ The top part will fold down to make the flap of the pencil case.

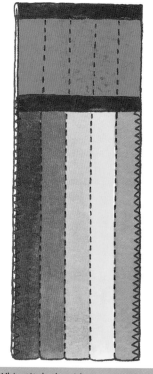

⚠ Whipstitch the sides, or use zigzag stitches.

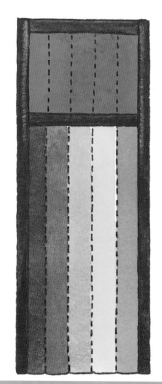

⚠ The bias binding and thread can be any color you choose.

7 Turn the fabric over so that the front of the pencil case is on the tabletop and the dark-colored lining is facing you. Fold up the bottom edge until it is about 3½ inches (9 cm) from the top. The top 3½ inches (9 cm) will be the flap of your pencil case.

8 Zigzag or whipstitch the two sides.

9 Bind the two sides with bias binding, making sure that the edges are folded over so that it is neat. (Turn to page 19 to see how to do this.) You could stitch on the bias binding with thread in a different color to make it more decorative.

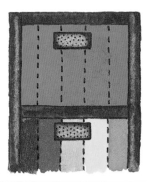

Adding Velcro or a small snap will stop the pencils from falling out.

10 Attach a small piece of Velcro or sew a small snap to the inside of the flap.

Tips

● If you don't have a white crayon, hardened soap is a good way of marking dark fabrics. When there is a little sliver of soap left, allow it to dry and harden. You can then use it like a crayon; it marks the fabric and can be rubbed off easily—and it smells nice!

● Instead of a thimble, put a piece of adhesive tape over your third finger when quilting; if your underneath finger is getting pricked, put a strip on that, too.

● If you happen to prick your finger and get blood on your work, don't panic; spit on another small piece of cloth and rub off the blood with it. It sounds nasty, but it works.

Variation

If you are using plain fabric for your pencil case, you can jazz it up with colorful quilting stitches.

Quilted picture cushion

Your mom and dad, or your grandparents, will just love this cushion with a picture drawn by you or your little sister or brother on it. A simple subject—such as a flower, or a cat, or a leaf—works best, as you need to stitch around the shape.

Materials

- Pencil
- Ruler
- 16 x 16 inches (40 x 40 cm) white, cream, or very pale-colored fabric for the front of the cushion
- Fabric crayons
- Old cotton pillowcase or paper towels
- Iron
- 16 x 16 inches (40 x 40 cm) fabric for the backing

- 16 x 16 inches (40 x 40 cm) batting
- Small quilting needle
- Safety pins
- White quilting or sewing thread
- Colored quilting or sewing thread
- Two pieces of fabric, the same color and size as the front, for the back of the cushion

How to make the quilted picture cushion

▲ Draw a pencil line around the fabric to make a "frame" for your picture.

1 Using a ruler and a pencil, draw a faint square around the pale-colored fabric for the front of the cushion, about 2½ inches (6 cm) from the edge. This forms a frame for your picture.

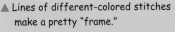

▲ Draw your picture with fabric crayons, which are specially made to use on fabric—so your picture won't fade or come off when you wash the cushion.

▲ Pin safety pins through all three layers to hold them together.

7 Continue adding lines of quilting, spacing them about ½ inch (1.25 cm) apart. The quilting makes the drawing stand out.

2 Using fabric crayons, draw a picture in the center of the fabric (or ask your brother or sister to draw one), making sure you don't draw over the pencil line. Fabric crayons can be a bit messy, so it's a good idea to practice on an old piece of fabric first.

3 Cover the drawing with an old cotton pillowcase or paper towels and iron it with a hot iron. (Ask an adult to help you.) This fixes the drawing, so that it won't come off the fabric.

4 Put the backing fabric flat on the table, with the batting on top of it, and the front of the cushion (on which you've drawn your picture) on top of the batting. Make sure the picture side faces upward.

5 Pin safety pins across the cushion at regular intervals, pinning through all three layers, or make large basting stitches from one side to the other and from top to bottom. Smooth down the fabric as you pin or baste, and check the back to see if there are any creases or crinkles. (The back will actually be inside the cushion, but it's good practice to make it nice and neat.) This holds the three layers together.

▲ Contour quilting—stitching around the shape—makes the picture stand out.

6 Thread your needle with white quilting or sewing thread and quilt around the outer line of your drawing. This is called contour quilting. If you find it hard to keep your stitches an even distance from the drawing, draw a faint pencil line around the drawing and stitch along the line.

▲ Lines of different-colored stitches make a pretty "frame."

8 Near the corners, where there's nothing drawn on the fabric, quilt diagonal lines. Quilt along the pencil line that you drew in step 1, to make a "frame" for your drawing. Four lines of quilting in different colors of thread look great.

Tip

To keep your thread from getting tangled while you're sewing, use the thread the way it came off the spool when threading your needle.

47

Cushion pieces

Your cushion pieces should be this shape. Follow the instructions below to make the cushion.

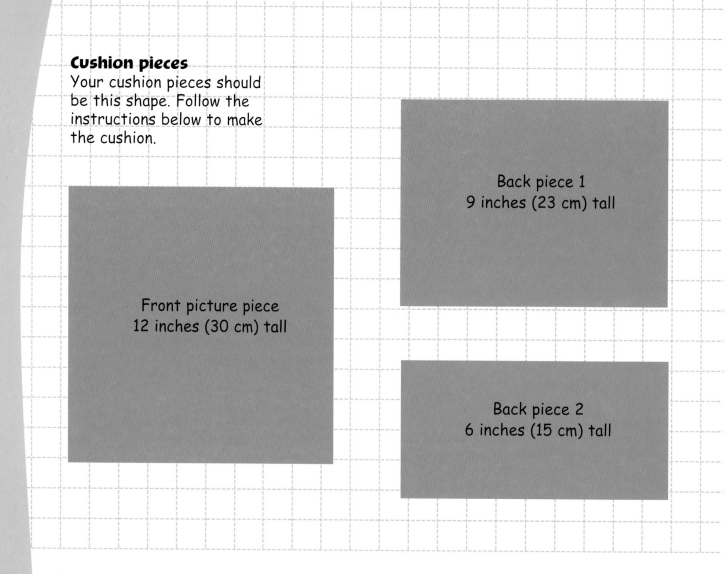

Back piece 1
9 inches (23 cm) tall

Front picture piece
12 inches (30 cm) tall

Back piece 2
6 inches (15 cm) tall

How to make the cushion

1 Measure your picture. It will be smaller than the 16 inches (40 cm) that you started with, as the quilting stitches pull the fabric in. Take a piece of fabric the same color as the front of the cushion, and cut a piece that is the same width as your picture and about three-quarters of the height of the picture—so if your picture is 12 inches (30 cm) tall, cut the fabric to 9 inches (23 cm). Make a hem across the width on one edge only.

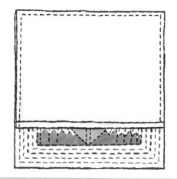

▲ Stitch around the three unhemmed sides to make the first part of the cushion flap.

2 Place this piece on top of your picture, with the right sides together and the unhemmed edge along the top of the picture. Machine-stitch around the three unhemmed sides, ¼ inch (0.6 cm) from the edge.

▲ The two pieces overlap, making an "envelope" into which you can put the cushion pad.

3 Cut another piece of fabric the same width as your picture and half the height—so if your picture is 12 inches (30 cm) tall, this new piece should be 6 inches (15 cm) tall. Again, make a hem across the width on one edge only. Place this piece on top of your picture and the previous piece, so that the unhemmed edge is along the bottom of your picture. Machine-stitch around the three unhemmed edges as before, stitching ¼ inch (0.6 cm) from the edge. You have made a kind of envelope for the cushion pad.

4 Turn the cushion cover right side out, put in a pillow form, and sit back and admire your work.

Did you know?

● Contour quilting is so called because it's like the contour lines on maps, which tell you how high the land is above sea level.

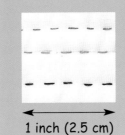

1 inch (2.5 cm)

● In the olden days, little girls were encouraged to make tiny, neat stitches and do five quilting stitches to the inch! Why not measure yours and see how many stitches you can do?

Shadow-quilted herb bag

This little herb bag is very quick to make and makes a lovely present. It can be filled with lavender or potpourri, and would be great to pop in a drawer to keep clothes smelling sweet. Shadow quilting is very easy to do. It's called shadow quilting because a brightly colored fabric is placed under some voile or net fabric, which makes the color look duller—as if it's in shadow. Maybe Mom has some old net curtains in a closet that you could use for this project— but always ask for permission before you cut up any household item. You can often find net curtains for sale in thrift stores.

Materials

- Two 6-inch (15-cm) squares of fabric
- Pinking shears and fabric scissors
- One 6-inch (15-cm) square of voile or net
- One 3-inch (7-cm) square of bright red or pink fabric
- Pencil
- Pins
- Needle
- Pink thread
- Paper
- Herbs or potpourri

How to make the shadow-quilted herb bag

▲ Cut the fabric with pinking shears. It looks pretty and stops the fabric from fraying.

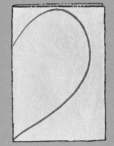

▲ Fold the red or pink fabric in half, and draw one half of the heart along the fold.

1 Cut two 6-inch (15-cm) squares of fabric with pinking shears. This makes a nice edge and won't fray.

2 Cut a 6-inch (15-cm) square of voile or net with the pinking shears.

3 Fold the pink or red fabric in half. Using a soft pencil, lightly draw half a heart shape on one side of the fold, then cut it out with fabric scissors. This ensures that each half of the heart will be exactly the same.

4 Place the heart in the middle of one square of fabric.

▲ Quilt a second line, ¹/₂ inch (1.25 cm) from the first.

7 Quilt another line around the heart ½ inch (1.25 cm) away from the first line of quilting.

8 Place the quilted front on top of the other square of fabric and pin it at the corners.

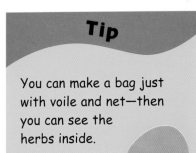

▲ Fill the bag with potpourri, and stitch the gap closed.

10 Fold some paper into a funnel and fill the bag with the herbs or potpourri. Sew up the gap to complete the bag.

▲ Place the heart in the middle of one fabric square, and pin the voile or net on top.

5 Place the square of voile or net on top of the heart, and pin it down at the corners. You will see that the heart now looks paler in color than it did before.

▲ Quilt around the edge of the heart.

6 Thread a needle with pink thread, and quilt around the outline of the heart, stitching through the voile and the fabric underneath. This will hold the heart in place and keep it from slipping.

▲ Stitch around the edges, leaving a gap in one side.

9 Quilt ½ inch (1.25 cm) away from the edge to join all the pieces of fabric together and make them into a bag, leaving a gap of 2 inches (5 cm) in one side so that you can fill the bag with herbs or potpourri.

Tip

You can make a bag just with voile and net—then you can see the herbs inside.

Circle quilt for teddy bear

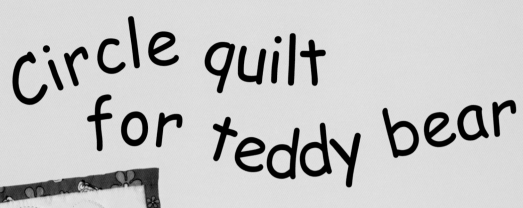

I expect you have a teddy bear or another toy that has a special place on your bed. Why not make him his very own quilt? It's a great way to learn how to quilt in circles and make up your own quilting designs. This is a very old quilting pattern, which has been used for centuries.

The size of the quilt depends on how big your teddy bear is. Measure him, and cut a piece of fabric that's big enough to cover him snugly.

How to make the circle quilt

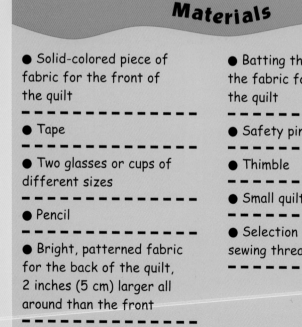

Materials

- Solid-colored piece of fabric for the front of the quilt

- Tape

- Two glasses or cups of different sizes

- Pencil

- Bright, patterned fabric for the back of the quilt, 2 inches (5 cm) larger all around than the front

- Batting the same size as the fabric for the front of the quilt

- Safety pins

- Thimble

- Small quilting needle

- Selection of colored sewing threads

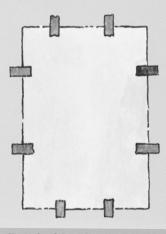

▲ Tape the fabric for the front of the quilt onto the table.

1 Stick the fabric for the front of the quilt to the table with some tape, so that it won't move around when you draw the circles.

Tip

You can use many different household items for drawing your circles. Why not try lids for jars, rolls of tape, food cans, cooking trays, or coasters?

▲ Make a "sandwich," with the batting in the middle.

4 Take off the tape, and make the quilt "sandwich." Put the patterned backing fabric right side down on the table and smooth out any wrinkles, place the batting in the middle of the backing fabric, and put the quilted front of the quilt right side up on top of the batting.

▲ Cups come in many different sizes. Don't choose a really small one.

2 Put a glass or cup upside down on the fabric, and draw around it with a soft pencil to make a circle.

▲ Cover the fabric in circles of different sizes, overlapping them in places.

3 Cover the fabric with circles, some of different sizes, but leave a border about 2 inches (5 cm) all around the edge. Where the circles overlap, they make a different shape—like the symbol for the Olympic Games.

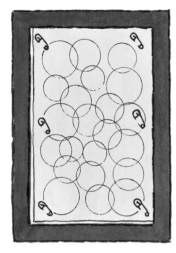

▲ Hold the layers together with safety pins.

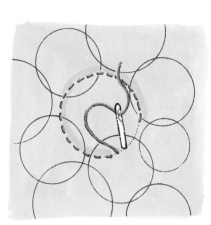

▲ Starting in the middle of your fabric, stitch around the circles.

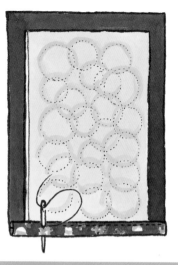

▲ Fold the backing over to the front, and stitch it in place.

5 Pin safety pins across the quilt at regular intervals, pinning through all three layers, or make large basting stitches from one side to the other and from top to bottom. Smooth down the fabric as you pin or baste, and check the back to make sure that there are no creases or crinkles.

6 Put a thimble on your middle finger, as you'll need to push hard to get the needle through all three layers of fabric. Thread your needle with a bright color of thread and, starting in the middle, quilt around a complete circle. To finish off, neatly bring the needle to the back, take a small stitch, and finish.

7 Continue quilting the circles, making each one a different color from its neighbor. Keep on turning the quilt over and checking that the back isn't getting creased.

8 Now bind the edges. Fold the backing fabric on the top and bottom edges over to the front, fold under the raw edge, and pin it in place. Then stitch along the edge to hold it down. Do the same thing on the sides of the quilt.

▲ Fold the corners neatly and secure the binding so that there are no holes.

9 When you come to the corners of the quilt, make sure the sides fold over neatly. Finish the stitches with a knot concealed in the work (see page 41).

Quilting

Tips

● Make a quilt like this for your little sister's dolls, or make a bigger quilt for a baby's crib.

● If you think circles are boring, raid the kitchen drawer and use cookie cutters as your template—you might even find one shaped like a teddy bear!

Appliqué and quilting techniques

Appliqué is a special word for fastening pieces of fabric, usually cut into pretty shapes, onto a backing fabric. You can use fancy stitches to hold the shapes in place: blanket stitch, feather stitch, herringbone stitch, and chain stitch all look very pretty (see page 16).

If you have a sewing machine that can do embroidery stitches, you can use them in the same way as the hand stitches. It's a lot of fun to play with different stitches, and you can even make them different sizes so that they give different effects.

If you change stitches on a sewing machine, always make sure you return the machine to the same stitch you started with. An adult might not be pleased to find they've sewn roses all over a shirt they were mending with a straight stitch!

Avoiding frayed edges

When you cut shapes out of cotton fabric, the edges can fray, so some of the projects in this section use appliqué shapes in felt or fleece, as these fabrics don't fray. They also come in bright colors and patterns.

If you are using cotton fabric, one way of preventing it from fraying is to turn under a hem on the shapes and then hem them onto the backing. A much easier method is to use fusible bonding web to stick the shapes to the background fabric.

Fussy cutting

This form of appliqué involves patterned fabric. If you have say, a teddy with some flowers, you can cut out the teddy bears and the flowers and apply them to different quilts. It's a way of making your work individual and a small piece of interesting fabric stretch further. This technique is also called broderie perse. In the olden days, chintz—a fabric with patterns of flowers and birds—was extremely expensive, so people bought small amounts of it, cut out the birds and flowers, and appliquéd them onto a larger piece of cheaper fabric: then they could decorate a whole bed quilt from one small bit of fabric! It's a clever idea, isn't it?

Using fusible bonding web

This is an easy way to fix your appliqué to the fabric, no sewing is needed, or, you could be clever and stick the shapes down and then add fancy stitches on top. There are many types of bonding web, and instructions may vary, so always read and follow the manufacturer's instructions.

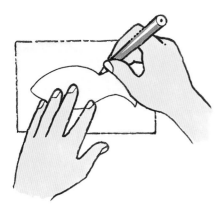

1 Trace or draw your shape onto the smooth side of the bonding web, remembering to reverse the design, so that it will appear the correct way when fastened onto your work.

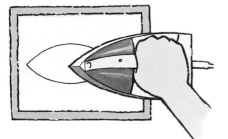

2 Put the rough (sticky) side of the bonding web on the back of the fabric that you've chosen to make your shapes from and, using a warm iron, iron the paper pieces in place. (You might want to ask an adult to help with this.) This will transfer the glue from the paper to the fabric.

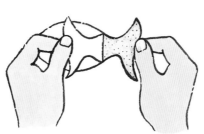

3 Cut out your shape accurately and peel off the backing paper. The fabric underneath the paper should be sticky.

4 Place your fabric shape on your chosen backing fabric, sticky side down, cover it with a damp cloth, and press it with a warm iron; it will stick firmly. You can even wash it in a machine and it won't come undone.

Quilting appliqué

When you've applied the shapes, you can make them stand out by contour quilting (see page 49) all around the outside, using thread the same color as the background fabric. If you have a solid-colored backing fabric, you will have a nice pattern of stitched shapes on the back. You can then use your quilt either way around! We've done this in Project 8, Circle Quilt for Teddy Bear.

Handy snuggle rug

This rug is made from fleece fabric, which is wonderfully soft and warm. You could have it on your bed or—even better—use it to snuggle up in while watching television. When you cut the fabric, it doesn't fray or go to pieces, so it's really easy to use. Because you are using your own handprints, it will be unique— no one else in the whole world will have one like it!

Materials

- Scrap paper
- Pencil
- Paper scissors
- 40 x 65 inches (102 x 165 cm) fleece fabric
- Small pieces of colored fleece or washable felt
- Ballpoint pen, crayon, or hard soap
- Fabric scissors
- Pins
- Large-eyed needle
- Brightly colored thread or 6-stranded embroidery floss

How to make the snuggle rug

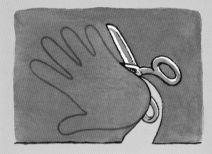

▲ Draw your shapes on paper and cut them out. Use these templates to make your fabric shapes.

1 Place your hand on the paper, with your fingers splayed out, and draw around it with the pencil. Do this again with your fingers tightly together but your thumb stretched out. Cut out the shapes with paper scissors—these are your patterns. Use these patterns to cut your fabric shapes, either by drawing around them onto the fabric, or pinning them to the fabric and cutting directly around them. You could draw around the different-sized hands of your family and friends (write on each pattern whose hand it is, in case you want to make them into pairs of wings later).

2 Put your large piece of fleece on a table or the floor, with the furry side up, and smooth it out. You can now cut out all of the shapes to be sewn onto it. When you cut out shapes and sew them onto a base, this is called appliqué.

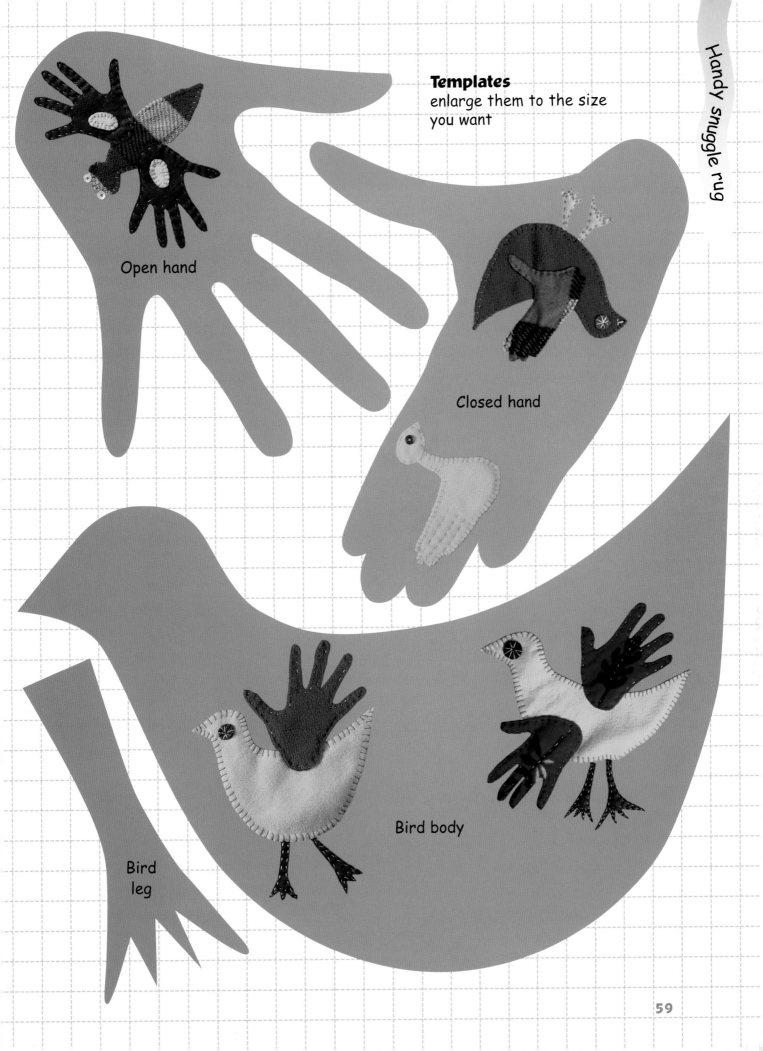

Templates
enlarge them to the size
you want

Open hand

Closed hand

Bird body

Bird
leg

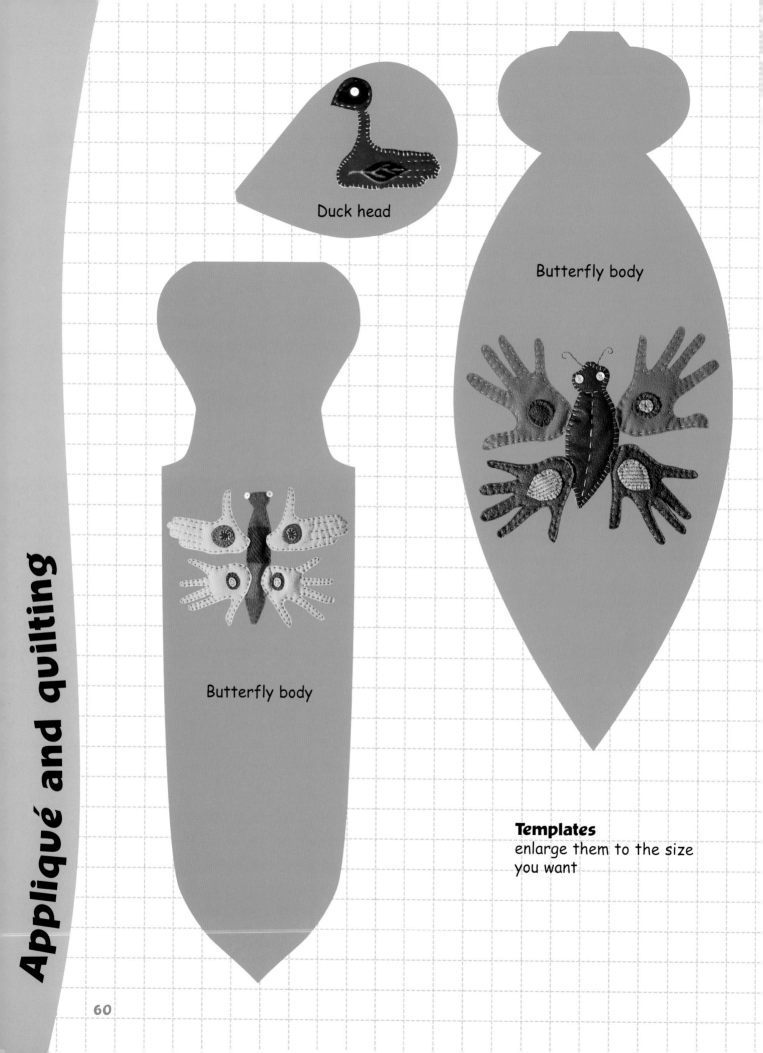

Duck head

Butterfly body

Butterfly body

Templates
enlarge them to the size
you want

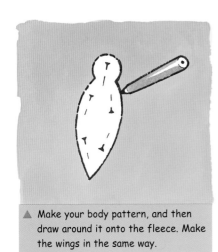

⚠ Make your body pattern, and then draw around it onto the fleece. Make the wings in the same way.

3 Butterflies To make the butterflies, trace a body shape from the previous page onto paper—there's a choice of two different body shapes. Cut out the shape and use this as your pattern. Pin the pattern to the wrong side of some bright fleece or felt (which isn't so furry), and draw around it with ballpoint pen, crayon, or hard soap. Cut out the shape of the body. Now cut two or four wings in another bright color—these are made from your open-fingered template. Place them on your rug.

4 Swan or duck To make a swan or duck, use the pattern that you made by drawing around the hand with shut fingers and a stretched-out thumb. Cut one fleece or felt shape and one head. Make the template by tracing around the drawing. You could even have a duck with a different-colored head and body. Place these on the rug.

5 Bird To make a bird, use the bird body and legs pattern and either one of the hand templates. Trace and make the template as before, and cut out a body, two legs, and one or two wings from the hand templates. Place on the rug.

6 Continue adding birds, ducks, and butterflies, or make up some weird-looking bugs! Move them around the rug until you like the pattern they make, spacing them evenly if you can.

Ready-made

You could use preprinted blankets for your quilt like the ones shown here (below left and right). Make sure they're made of fleece or felt—then all you need to do is cut out the shapes and you have instant decorations!

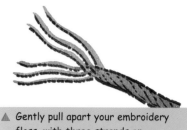

▲ Gently pull apart your embroidery floss, with three strands on either side.

8 If you are using embroidery floss, it must be halved into three strands in each half. Cut a length of thread, then spread it between your fingers—at the edge you will see there are six strands. Pull three strands in each hand and it will divide into two lengths of thread. It is easier to sew with and you get twice as much from each skein of thread, saving money, so you can buy more colors!

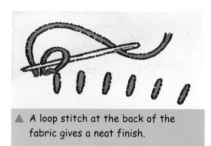

▲ A loop stitch at the back of the fabric gives a neat finish.

9 To finish off neatly, take the thread to the back, make a small stitch (but leave a loop) then bring the needle through the loop and pull it tight—this makes a neat knot. Do it twice to make sure it isn't going to come undone.

▲ Pass the needle in and out, making stitches of equal length.

7 Pin the patches to the fleece and sew each one with either a running stitch (above) or the blanket stitch from page 16 (this was used to stop blankets from fraying before we had comforters on our beds). Sew with a large-eyed needle so that you can thread it easily, and use different-colored threads.

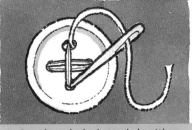

▲ Sew through the buttonhole with an "X," going back over it several times.

10 For the finishing touch, you can add buttons for eyes and sew some antennae onto the butterflies. Be as inventive as you like!

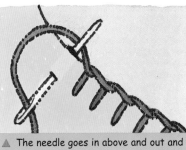

▲ The needle goes in above and out and over the thread for blanket stitch.

11 Blanket stitch all the way around to finish off the edge. Finish neatly, using the technique you learned in step 9.

Sweatshirt portrait

This is a fun way of making your own designer sweatshirt—you can be sure no one else will have one the same as yours. You could make a portrait of yourself, one of your friends, or even your entire family. The fun is seeing if they recognize who's who! You can add buttons for eyes, embroider a smiling mouth, make hair from braids of frayed fabric, put ribbons in the hair, stitch on beads or old bits of jewelry—the amount of detail you include is entirely up to you.

Materials

- Pencil
- Skin-colored fabric
- Iron
- Fusible webbing
- Fabric scissors
- An old sweatshirt
- Needle
- Red embroidery floss
- Two buttons for eyes
- Scraps of hair-colored fabric or knitting yarn
- Thread the same color as the hair
- Fabric for body
- Beads, buttons, sequins, or other decorations of your choice

How to make the sweatshirt portrait

Draw a face shape on the wrong side of some skin-colored fabric.

Stick the face to the sweatshirt with fusible web.

1 Using a soft pencil, draw a face shape with a neck on the wrong side of your skin-colored fabric.

2 Iron some fusible webbing onto the wrong side of the drawing, using a dry iron over the paper side of the webbing. This will transfer the glue from the webbing to the fabric. (You may want to get an adult to help you.) Cut around the drawn line.

3 Peel off the paper from the fusible web and place it on the front of the sweatshirt, then iron the fabric to stick it onto the sweatshirt. (You may want to ask an adult to help with this.)

4 Draw a mouth on the face and embroider over the pencil lines with chain stitch, using red embroidery floss. (Turn to page 16 to see how to do chain stitch.)

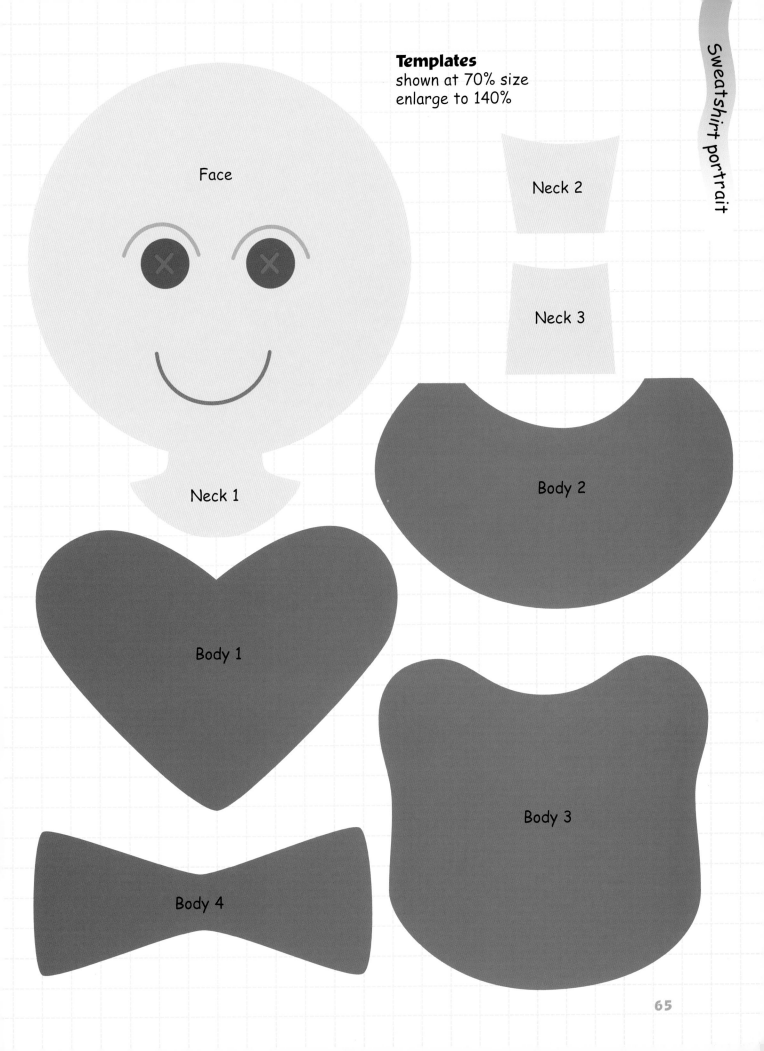

Face

Templates
shown at 70% size
enlarge to 140%

Neck 2

Neck 3

Neck 1

Body 2

Body 1

Body 3

Body 4

△ A chain-stitch mouth and button eyes complete the face.

△ Stitch on strips of torn fabric for the hair. Tie braids with ribbon.

5 Draw two dots for the eyes, and sew on the two buttons (see page 19). By now your portrait should be starting to look like a real person.

7 Thread a needle with thread the same color as the hair, and sew the strips of fabric to the head, using small quilting stitches. If you want to braid the hair, sew just one end of the strips to the head and leave the rest loose. When you've braided the hair, secure the ends with ribbon or elastic bands to keep them from unraveling.

△ Sew the hair onto the head with the same color thread.

△ Cut a big heart or rounded oblong for the body shape.

6 Now make the hair. Tear up some strips of fabric in your chosen hair color— yellow, brown, black, or maybe even shocking pink! Tearing the strips will make them fray, so that they look more hairy. For short hair, tear strips about 4 inches (10 cm) long; for long hair or braids, tear strips about 15 inches (38 cm) long. If you prefer, you can use knitting yarn.

8 Now make the body. Draw a body shape—a rounded oblong, or a heart—on the back of your body fabric, iron on some fusible webbing to the wrong side of your drawing, like you did earlier, and then cut around the shape you've drawn. Peel off the paper from the fusible webbing, and iron the body onto the front of the sweatshirt. (Again, you might want to ask an adult to help with this.)

9 Now you can add some decoration to the body. Here are some ideas that you might like to try.

Stick or stitch on a necklace of beads and sequins.

Stitch on a lace collar or a row of buttons.

Fussy cut around a picture of a teddy bear or cat and bond it onto the body.

Write your name, or the name of your school, in fabric crayons.

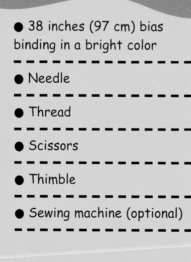

Jazzy bag

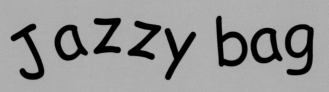

This great-looking shoulder bag is made by stitching colorful ribbons at an angle onto a piece of fabric. Ribbons are great to work with, because they don't fray, and they come in different widths and lots of different colors. This bag is 10 inches (25 cm) deep, but you can make it any size you want—smaller for a change purse, or bigger for carrying schoolbooks.

How to make the jazzy bag

▲ Place the batting between the bag fabric and the lining, to make a "sandwich."

1 Make a "sandwich," with the batting in between the two pieces of fabric. Put the lining fabric right side down on the table, with the batting on top of it, and the front of the bag on top of the batting.

▲ Fix the layers together with safety pins.

2 Pin safety pins across the "sandwich," pinning through all three layers to hold them together.

Materials

- 7 x 20 inches (18 x 50 cm) fabric for the front of the bag
- 7 x 20 inches (18 x 50 cm) fabric for the lining
- 7 x 20 inches (18 x 50 cm) batting
- Safety pins
- Sewing pins
- Selection of brightly colored ribbons

- 38 inches (97 cm) bias binding in a bright color
- Needle
- Thread
- Scissors
- Thimble
- Sewing machine (optional)

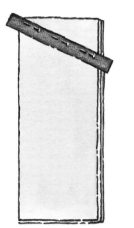

▲ Pin the ribbon onto the fabric at an angle.

3 Using normal sewing pins, pin the first ribbon across the fabric at an angle; this leaves a triangle at the top, which will be filled in later.

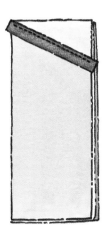

▲ Sew as close to the edge of the ribbon as you can.

4 Sew the ribbon to the fabric underneath, by stitching along the top edge of the ribbon. Stitch through all three layers of fabric. You can use either a machine, or, if you prefer sewing by hand, running stitches.

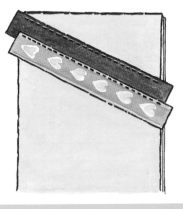

▲ Overlap the second ribbon on the first, and stitch it on in the same way.

5 Pin the next ribbon in place, overlapping it on the first ribbon by about ¼ inch (0.6 cm), and stitch it in place in the same way. The great thing about ribbons is that they don't fray, so you don't have to turn under the edge.

6 Continue adding ribbons in the same way, varying the width of the ribbons and the colors to make it look really pretty. As you sew, smooth down the layers with your hand and check the back to make sure there are no puckers or creases.

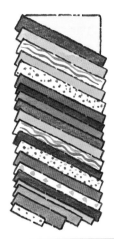

▲ When you get to the bottom of the fabric, fill in the empty triangle at the top with ribbons.

7 When you reach the bottom of the fabric, go back and add extra ribbons at the top to fill in the triangle shape.

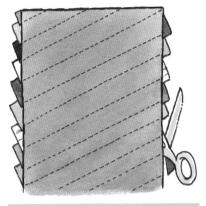

▲ Trim the ribbons so that they're level with the edges of the fabric.

8 Trim off any bits of ribbon that stick out over the edges of the fabric.

▲ Bind the top and bottom with colorful bias binding.

9 Take out the safety pins, and bind the top and bottom edges with bias binding. (Turn to page 19 to see how to do this.) Choose a bright color of binding that goes well with the ribbons.

No ribbons? Use strips of brightly colored fabric instead. Sew them in a method called Flip and Sew.

▲ Place the first fabric strip right side down on the fabric, and stitch along the bottom edge.

▲ Fold or flip the fabric strip along the stitched line so that it's right side up.

▲ Place the next fabric strip on top of the first, right sides together, overlapping them by about ¼ inch (0.6 cm), and stitch and flip as before.

▲ Fold the piece in half, with the ribbons on the outside.

10 Fold the fabric in half lengthwise, so that the ribbons are on the outside.

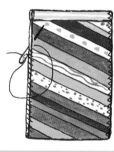

▲ Stitch up the sides of the bag to close them.

11 Using a zigzag stitch if you're sewing by machine, or whipstitching if you're sewing by hand, sew up the sides of the bag.

12 Bind the sides with bias binding to cover up the stitches, remembering to turn under the top and bottom edges of the binding to make it really neat.

▶ In this variation, the ribbons are woven to create a pattern.

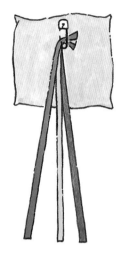

▲ Pin the ends of the ribbons to a cushion to hold them in place while you braid.

13 Measure across your shoulder with a tape measure to figure out how long you want the handle to be. It's a good idea to get someone to help you do this. Cut three pieces of ribbon 2 inches (5 cm) longer than you want the handle to be, and braid them together. You'll need to use both hands for braiding, so pin the three ribbons together at the top with a safety pin, and then pin the safety pin to a cushion so it's held firmly in place while you work—or get a friend to hold the ends for you.

▲ Snip the loose ends of ribbon below the stitches to make a tassel.

14 Sew across all three ribbons 1 inch (2.5 cm) from each end, or machine-stitch them with zigzag stitches. This keeps all your work from unraveling. Cut the loose ends of ribbon into strips to make a tassel.

15 Sew the handle securely to the bag at the top where the side binding covers the seams. Use a thimble to do this, as you need to push the needle through several layers of fabric, or get an adult to help you. Leave the tassels hanging loose.

Elephant quilt

This quilt was designed by Miriam Edwards and made by a group of girls who are in a club called the Young Quilters. Maybe there is a quilt club near you, or maybe you could start one with some friends. It's always nice to get together with friends and swap bits of fabric and share new ideas.

These elephants would look great on your bedroom wall. You could get all your friends to make an elephant for you and sign their names to make a very special quilt into a kind of autograph book.

Materials

FOR A 12-BLOCK QUILT:

● 24 x 24 inches (60 x 60 cm) cream fabric for the background

● Pencil

● Scissors

● Tracing paper and cardboard, or template plastic

● Fusible bonding web

● Iron

● 21 x 28 inches (53 x 71 cm) blue fabric for the elephants

● Brightly colored embroidery floss

● 12-inch (30-cm) square of glittery fabric for the ears

● Needle

● Thread

● Beads or buttons for eyes, sequins, and other decorations of your choice

● Yarn or thin ribbon for tails

● 4 x 32 inch (10 x 81 cm) bright green fabric for the strips between the elephants

● Bar soap

● Sewing machine

● Approx. 36 x 38 inches (91 x 96.5 cm) batting

● Approx. 40 x 42 inches (102 x 107 cm) backing fabric

How to make the elephant quilt

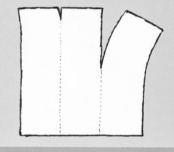

⚠ Rip or cut across the cream fabric every 8 inches (20 cm), so that you have three long strips.

1 On the cream fabric, make a pencil mark 8 inches (20 cm) in from one edge. Do the same thing 8 inches (20 cm) from the first mark. Make a small cut on each pencil mark and rip the fabric all the way across. (If you prefer, you could draw pencil lines and cut along them—but ripping the fabric is more fun!) You now have three strips measuring 8 x 24 inches (20 x 60 cm).

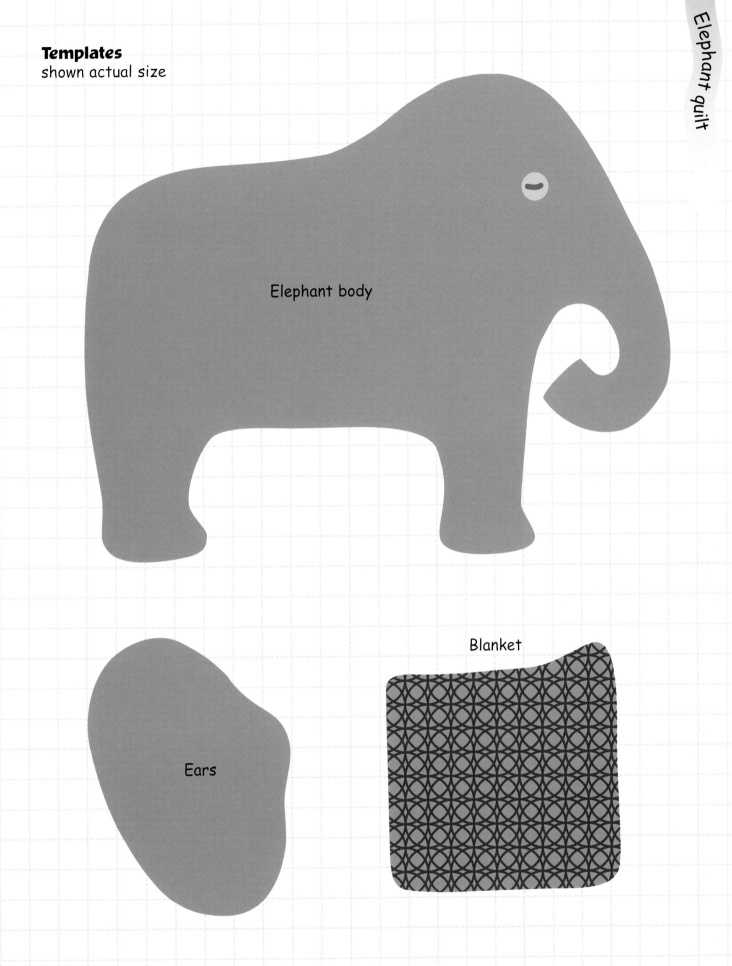

Templates
shown actual size

Elephant body

Ears

Blanket

▲ On each cream strip, make marks 6 inches (15 cm) apart along one long edge. Rip or cut as before, to make 12 rectangles.

2 Take the first strip and make pencil marks 6 inches (15 cm) apart along one long side. Make a small cut on each pencil mark, just as you did in step 1, and rip or cut across the fabric. Do the same thing with the other two long strips of cream fabric. You now have 12 rectangles measuring 6 x 8 inches (15 x 20 cm) on which to place your elephants.

3 Trace the elephant template on page 73 onto template plastic, or onto tracing paper and glue the tracing onto a piece of cardboard from a cereal box or old greetings card. Carefully cut around the edge of the elephant tracing—you now have a template.

4 Iron fusible bonding web onto the back of the blue fabric. (You might want to ask an adult to help you.)

5 Place your elephant template on the bonding web and draw around it 12 times. If you like, you can turn the template over for some of the drawings, so that some elephants are looking to the right and some are looking to the left. Cut around your drawings so that you have 12 elephants.

▲ Take the paper off the back of the elephant shapes, place each one in the middle of a piece of cream fabric, and press with a warm iron.

6 Take the paper backing off the bonding web and place each elephant, fabric side up, in the middle of a piece of cream fabric. Press with a warm iron (or ask an adult to do this for you)—the heat will stick the elephants to the cream background.

▲ Decorate each elephant with brightly colored stitches.

7 If you like, for decoration sew around each elephant in blanket stitch as shown on page 16, using a brightly colored embroidery floss.

8 Trace the pattern for the ear and make a template from cardboard or template plastic, just as you did for the body of the elephant in step 3.

9 You need to make 12 ears—one for each elephant. Put your template on the back of some glittery fabric and draw around it 12 times, then do the same thing on the back of some blue fabric.

10 Cut out the ears, cutting about ¼ inch (0.6 cm) outside the drawn line. (The drawn line is the line that you will sew along.)

▲ Whipstitch one edge of the ear to the elephant's body, leaving the rest of it free to flap around.

11 Take one ear in glittery fabric and one in blue fabric and put them together so that the pencil lines are on the outside. Using small running stitches (see page 15), sew along the pencil line, leaving a gap of about 1¼ inches (3 cm) on the edge that will be stitched onto the elephant. Turn the ear right side out, fold in the unstitched bits of fabric along the gap, and overstitch this part of the ear to the elephant's body. Make and attach the remaining ears in the same way.

12 Trace the pattern for the blanket and make a template from cardboard or template plastic, just as you did for the body of the elephant in step 3.

Appliqué and quilting

13 Iron a piece of fusible bonding web onto the wrong side of a piece of brightly colored or glittery fabric. (Ask an adult to help.) Trace the blanket template onto the bonding web and cut out the shape. Peel the backing paper off the bonding web, place the blanket on the elephant, and press with a warm iron to stick the blanket in place. (Remember to lift up the elephant's ear before you do this, so that you don't stick it down by mistake!)

▲ Decorate each elephant with beads, sequins, or anything else you like.

14 Now decorate the elephants: you might decide to sew or glue on a bead for the eye, beads or sequins around the feet, or fringe on the blanket, but try to make each elephant different.

▲ Braid three strands of colored yarn or ribbon to make a tail.

15 Take three strands of colored yarn or narrow ribbon and braid them together to make a tail. Sew a tail onto each elephant.

Sashing the quilt

This is a way of joining up lots of small blocks or pictures to make them into a larger quilt. You can use this method for any quilt or wall hanging. It might seem hard at first, but with some help from an adult, you will manage it just fine.

1 Cut a strip of the bright green fabric measuring 4 x 32 inches (10 x 81 cm). Fold it in half, and either cut or tear it to make two strips measuring 2 x 32 inches (5 x 81 cm).

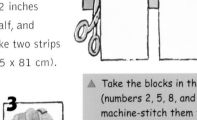

1	**2**	**3**
4	**5**	**6**
7	**8**	**9**
10	**11**	**12**

▲ Lay the elephant blocks out in four rows of three on the table or floor, and number them.

2 Place your elephants on a table or on the floor in four rows of three elephants. Remember, you might have some looking to the left and some to the right, so you might need to move them around until you're happy with how they look. Number each block with bar soap, or in pencil, near the edge of the fabric so that you can remember which one goes where when you begin to sew the blocks together.

▲ Take the blocks in the middle row (numbers 2, 5, 8, and 11), and machine-stitch them to a green fabric strip, leaving a gap between each one.

3 Put one green fabric strip faceup under the machine and put the first elephant of the middle row (block number 2) facedown so that the short edge lines up with the edge of the green strip. Machine-stitch the two pieces together, stitching about ¼ inch (0.6 cm) from the edge. Leave a small gap and then stitch the next elephant block (block number 5) to the green fabric in the same way. Stitch on blocks 8 and 11 in the same way. This is called continuous piecing—it is a quick way of joining the blocks.

▲ Trim the green fabric so that it is level with the edge of each elephant block, and press the seam open.

4 Cut the pieces apart, trimming the green fabric so that it is level with the edge of each elephant block, and press the seam open.

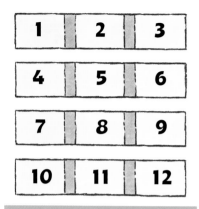

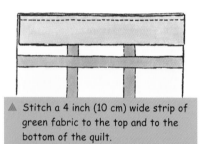

line up, and machine-stitch about ¼ inch (0.6 cm) from the edge. Now machine-stitch the other side of this strip to the top of the second row (the heads of blocks 4, 5, and 6). Sew the second green strip to the bottom of 4, 5, and 6 and to the top of blocks 7, 8, and 9. Finally, sew the third green strip to the bottom of blocks 7, 8, and 9 and the top of blocks 10, 11, and 12. (Aren't you glad you numbered the blocks before you started?!) Good job—you've learned how to sash a quilt!

▲ Now each elephant in this row has a bright green strip on each side of it.

▲ Stitch the elephant blocks on the outer edge of each row to the green strips of the middle row.

5 Take the other strip of green fabric and do the same to the other side of the blocks in the middle row.

7 Take block number 1 and put it facedown on top of block number 2 (faceup), lining it up with the edge of the green strip. Machine-stitch the two pieces together, stitching ¼ inch (0.6 cm) from the edge. Place block number 3 facedown on the other side of block number 2 (faceup), lining it up with the edge of the green strip, and machine-stitch in the same way. Press open the seams. Stitch the second, third, and fourth rows together in the same way. You now have four strips of three elephants each.

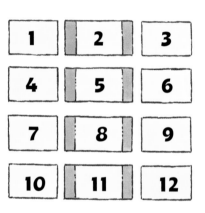

▲ Put the middle row of elephants back on the table.

6 Put the elephants back in their rows on the table.

▲ Stitch a 4 inch (10 cm) wide strip of green fabric to the top and to the bottom of the quilt.

9 To finish the quilt, you need to add more sashing strips all around the edges. Cut two strips of the bright green fabric measuring 4 x 28 inches (10 x 71 cm). Right sides together, place one strip along the top of the quilt, making sure the edges line up, and machine-stitch about ¼ inch (0.6 cm) from the edge to join the pieces together. Press the seam open. Sew the second strip to the bottom of the quilt in the same way.

10 Cut two green fabric strips measuring 4 x 38 inches (10 x 96.5 cm) and sew one to each side of the quilt, in the same way as you did in step 9.

▲ Stitch a long strip of green fabric between each row.

8 Cut three more strips of the bright green fabric, measuring 2 x 28 inches (5 x 71 cm). Put one strip right side down along the bottom of the first row, making sure the edges

▲ Now stitch a 4 inch (10 cm) wide strip of green fabric to each side of the quilt.

11 Cut a piece of batting the same size as the quilt (roughly 36 x 38 inches [91 x 96.5 cm]) and a piece of backing fabric 2 inches (5 cm) larger all the way around (roughly 40 x 42 inches [102 x 107 cm]). Make a "sandwich" by putting the backing fabric right side down on the table, with the batting centered on top of it, and the quilt top right side up on top of the batting. Pin safety pins through all three layers to hold the fabrics together. Quilt along each strip of sashing using green thread.

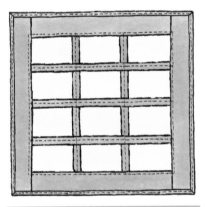

▲ Fold the backing fabric over to the front of the quilt, and stitch it in place.

12 Fold over the back edge to the front and quilt down as we did in Project 8 Circle Quilt for Teddy Bear, on page 54.

Note

An adult quilted the quilt made by the girls on the machine, and added an extra row sewn on with buttons. Maybe you can find someone who would like to quilt yours!

Swimming bag

How about making yourself a stylish swimming bag lined with plastic, so that your wet swimsuit won't drip on other things? You can cut a strong plastic shopping bag to the right size, or buy a plastic sheet from a hardware store.

A smaller version of the bag would be perfect for your toothbrush and toiletries when you visit your friends for a sleepover. This bag has swimsuit shapes on one side and snorkeling teddy bears on the other—if you want to decorate your bag with swimsuits, trace the pictures on the next page. Or choose your own pictures from preprinted fabrics: quilt stores sell small pieces of fabric, called "quarters," that are ideal for projects like this—and you may even find nice pictures on old clothes that you've grown out of.

Materials

- White crayon or bar soap
- Ruler
- 26 x 20 inches (66 x 50 cm) dark blue fabric
- 24 x 20 inches (60 x 50 cm) batting
- 24 x 20 inches (60 x 50 cm) plastic
- Sewing machine
- Pins
- Patterned fabric
- Scraps of striped and dotted fabric
- Bonding web
- Pencil
- Scissors
- Sewing machine
- Large-eyed needle
- Embroidery floss in bright colors
- 35 inches (89 cm) thin ribbon
- Safety pin

How to make the swimming bag

1 Using a light-colored crayon or bar soap and a ruler, draw a line along one long edge of the dark blue fabric, 2 inches (5 cm) from the top. This will be the folded-over top of the bag.

78

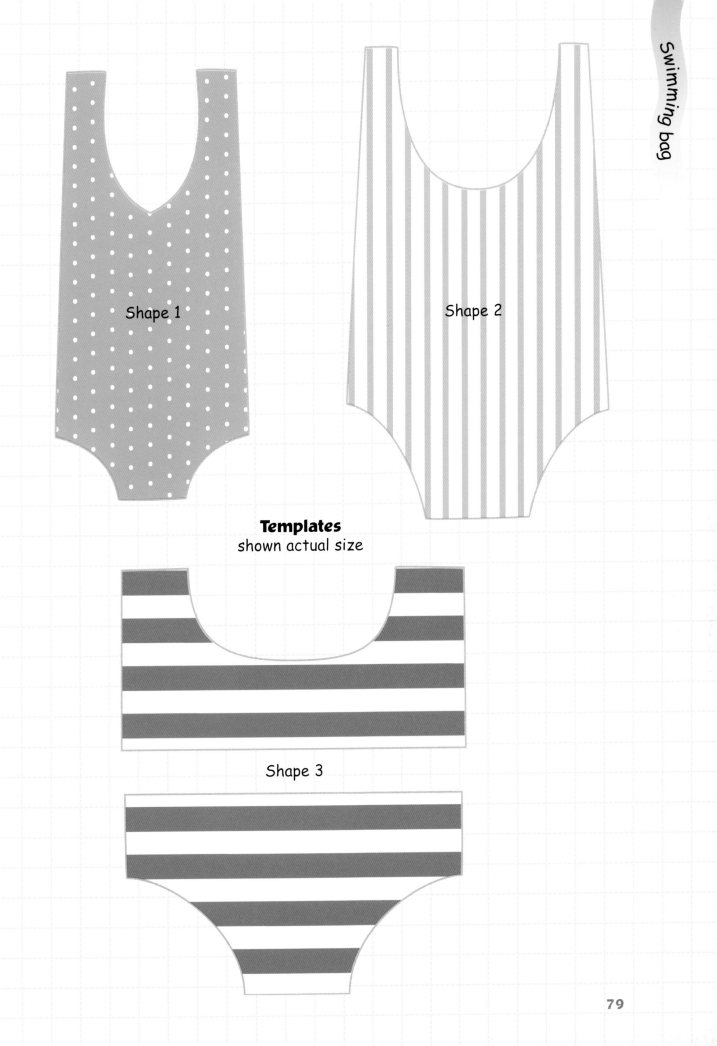

Shape 1

Shape 2

Templates
shown actual size

Shape 3

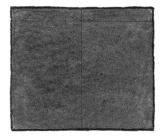

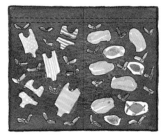

▲ Draw a line along one long edge, 2 inches (5 cm) from the top, and another down the center of the fabric.

▲ Fold the blue fabric over the plastic and batting, and stitch in place.

▲ Make ties all over the bag, 1 inch (2.5 cm) apart.

2 Fold the fabric in half widthwise, then open it up again and draw a faint line down the fold line. This shows you which part will be the front of the bag and which part will be the back.

4 Place the batting against the line that you drew in step 1, and place the plastic on top of the batting. Fold over 2 inches (5 cm) of the blue fabric so that it covers the batting and the plastic, and then turn under a ¼ inch (0.6 cm). Pin the folded-over fabric in place and sew it down with the machine. It's easier to sew through the plastic with a machine, but if you don't have a machine, just use a softer plastic bag and sew by hand.

6 The next stage is to quilt the bag. It's quite difficult to sew through plastic, so we're going to use tie quilting (see Seashore Scenes Quilt page 22), which also adds texture to the bag. Thread a large-eyed needle with brightly-colored embroidery floss or thick thread. Push the needle through all three layers, leaving about 1 inch (2.5 cm) of floss sticking out on the decorated fabric side. Then bring the needle back through the batting and plastic, so that both threads are on top of the work. Tie the threads with a reef knot, then cut the ends to about ½ inch (1.25 cm). Make ties roughly 1 inch (2.5 cm) apart, all over the bag.

▲ Bond your cut-out shapes to the background fabric.

▲ Sew a line ½ inch (1.25 cm) above the previous line.

7 Fold the bag in half widthwise, with the right sides together (so that the plastic is on the outside). Make sure the top edges line up, and pin the layers together, starting from the top of the bag.

3 Now you've got a nice big area to decorate as you wish. You can either trace the swimsuits on page 79 to make a template and draw around the template on striped and dotted fabric, or find preprinted fabrics with pictures of animals, birds, fish, or other subjects, to fussy cut (see page 56). Whichever you choose, back the fabric pictures with bonding web and iron them onto the fabric.

5 Now sew another line about ½ inch (1.25 cm) above the line you have just sewn. This makes the channel for the drawstring ribbon.

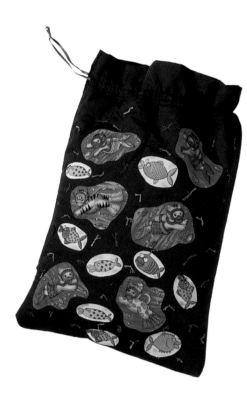

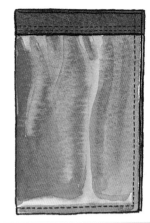

⚠ Cut a small slit on each side of the seam.

9 Turn the bag right side out. All you need now is the drawstring top. At the top of the bag, where you stitched the drawstring channel in step 5, make a little slit on each side of the seam with some small scissors. Make sure the slits are within the channel. You might want help with this; after all, you don't want to make a hole right through the bag after all that hard work!

⚠ Fold the bag in half widthwise, right sides together, and machine-stitch along the bottom and side, ¼ inch (0.6 cm) from the edge.

8 Stitching about ¼ inch (0.6 cm) from the edge, machine-stitch down the side and the bottom to complete the bag. Sometimes the plastic slips a little when you're doing this, so you might want to ask an adult to help you. A good tip to keep this from happening is to put some scrap paper over the plastic and stitch through the paper, then gently tear off the paper when all the stitching has been done.

⚠ Thread a ribbon through the channel and tie the loose ends.

10 Fasten a safety pin to the end of the ribbon and thread the ribbon through the channel. Remove the safety pin and tie the two ends of the ribbon, so that they can't disappear inside the channel. Pull up the drawstring, put your swimsuit in the bag, and you're ready for a trip to the pool.

3-D and trapunto techniques

So far, we've been stitching on flat pieces of fabric and then turning them into things such as bags and cushions—but there are also some really fun 3-D projects. There are even some simple ways of padding out parts of your design so that it's raised up from the surface.

3-D projects

Some of the projects, like the ladybug and bee pincushions and the pentagon ball, are stuffed to make them round, like balls. In other projects, only a small part is 3-D, such as the ears on the elephant quilt (pages 72–77): they're made separately and then stitched on.

For both types of 3-D projects, we've used fluffed batting for the stuffing. To do this, get some leftover bits of batting and pull at them until they're soft, like cotton balls. If you don't have any batting, use cotton balls, which you can buy in craft or drug stores.

When you're making 3-D objects, you need to make sure that your stitches are really firm so that the stuffing can't come out.

Teased-out batting and cotton balls

Trapunto

When just one part of the design is stuffed with batting to make it stand out, it's called trapunto. Trapunto is an Italian word that means "to embroider." The method began in the 1500s in Italy and was used on clothes to make them warm and for decoration. It was also very popular in Tudor England and was used for bags and purses and for little 3-D embroideries, which you can now see in some museums. Try the following projects and you will be carrying on a very old quilting tradition.

Front

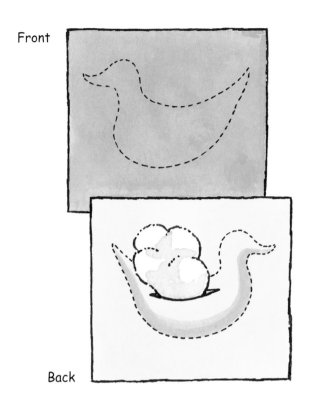

Back

Front

Front

Back

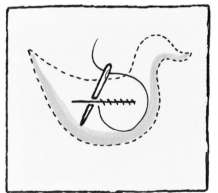

1 There are two ways of doing trapunto. The first method is to stuff batting into the work from the front, which is what we do in Project 16, Fancy Needle Book. The way to do this is to sew the shape that you want to pad out (in this case, the bird) onto the background fabric, leaving a small gap; then stuff fluffed batting into the bird, pushing it in with your fingers or the tip of a pencil. When the bird looks nice and fat, sew up the gap.

2 If you want to stuff areas that have already been quilted, you have to stuff them from the back. This method involves cutting a hole in the back of the work into which you poke the stuffing. You then have to sew up the hole, so this method involves a bit more work.

83

Laughing ladybug pincushion

A pincushion is very useful and easy to make. This one is a red-and-black ladybug, but you could invent your own—why not make one with wild colors, like a purple one with yellow spots? You could make lots of different bugs to give to all your friends who sew, and make them look really scary by using glass-topped pins for the eyes. You need only a few small scraps of fabric, so use pieces of felt or fleece left over from other projects.

Materials

- Tracing paper and cardboard, or template plastic

- Pencil

- Scissors

- White crayon or hard soap

- 4 x 10 inches (10 x 25 cm) red felt

- 4 x 4 inches (10 x 10 cm) black felt

- Thimble

- Thick red sewing thread

- Needle

- Scrap of blue felt for the eyes

- Batting for stuffing

How to make the ladybug pincushion

1 Trace the pattern for the body onto tracing paper, then cut out the tracing and glue it onto cardboard—or trace the pattern onto template plastic and cut out the shape. Trace the head in the same way.

3 Draw around the head pattern twice on black felt and cut out the shapes.

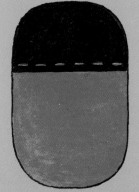

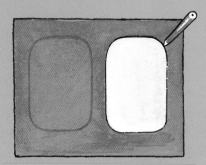

▲ Draw around the template twice, using white crayon or hard soap.

▲ Using big-stitch quilting stitches, sew one head part to each body part.

2 Using a white crayon or a piece of hard soap, draw around the body pattern twice on the red felt and cut out the shapes.

4 Using thick red thread and big-stitch quilting stitches, sew one head part to each body part.

Templates
shown actual size

Body

Trace the patterns for the
head and body and make
templates.

Head

⚠ Cut out spots, eyes, and a thin strip
of felt to go down the center of
the body.

5 Cut about nine squares of black
felt, in different sizes, for the spots
and trim them to make circles. Cut two
circles of blue felt for the eyes, and two
very small circles of black felt for the
pupils of the eyes. Cut a strip of black
felt 3 inches (7.5 cm) long and about
¼ inch (0.6 cm) wide.

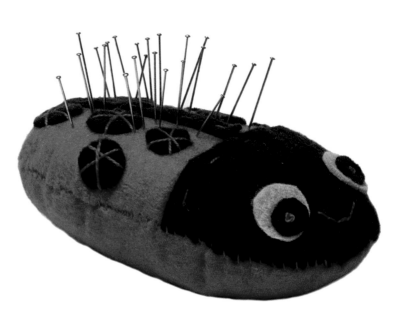

▲ Stitch the spots and eyes in place, and stitch a big, smiling mouth.

6 Now you can start to assemble your ladybug. Look at the drawing to see where the pieces go. Wearing a thimble and using red thread and big-stitch quilting, sew the black felt strip down the center of one body part. Stitch the spots to the body with a cross-stitch. Put the small black circle on top of the blue circle and sew down with a few stitches in a contrasting embroidery floss. Finally, stitch on a smiling mouth with some straight stitches.

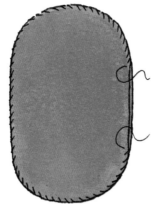

▲ Right sides together, whipstitch one head-and-body part to the other, leaving a 3 inch (7.5 cm) gap.

7 Now your ladybug's ready to be sewn together. Put the decorated side facedown on the other head-and-body part that you made in step 4, and whipstitch all the way around, leaving a gap of about 3 inches (7.5 cm).

▲ Turn the bug right side out and stuff with batting.

8 Turn the bug right side out. Stuff with batting until it's nice and fat, then sew up the gap. The bug's ready to hold your pins.

Want to make a busy bee pincushion?

1 Make the body template, as in step 1 of the ladybug, and make the stripe templates in the same way.

2 Draw around the template twice on yellow felt and cut out the shapes.

3 Draw around each stripe template once on black felt and cut the shapes out.

4 Follow step 5 of the ladybug instructions to make the eyes and the mouth.

5 Assemble, stitch, and stuff the bee in the same way as the ladybug, following steps 6, 7, and 8, but add the three black stripes instead of the spots and center strip.

⚠ Draw around the template to make the wings, then stick them in place using your pins.

6 To make the wings, make the template and cut out of yellow felt. Pin them to the body, either flat, or pinched at the narrow part so that they will stick up, ready to fly away. You can use the wings to store your needles.

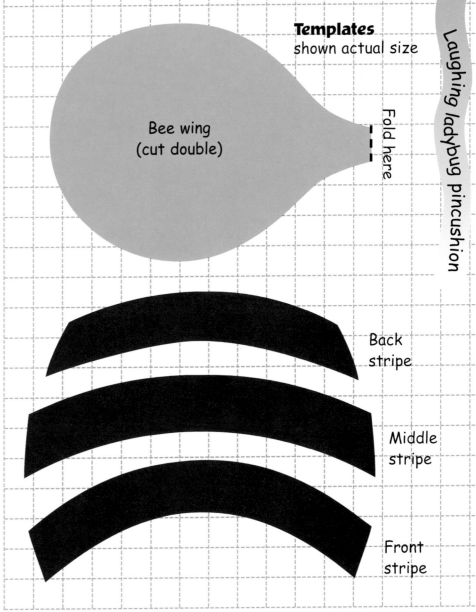

Templates shown actual size

Bee wing
(cut double)

Fold here

Back stripe

Middle stripe

Front stripe

Pentagon ball

Did you know that pentagon means "five sided?" This ball is made out of 12 pentagon-shaped pieces of felt. Hang it above a baby's crib as a colorful mobile, or make it for yourself and practice your ball skills in the house without breaking anything!

How to make the pentagon ball

1 Carefully trace the pentagon pattern onto tracing paper, then glue it to cardboard—or trace it onto template plastic—and cut it out. Try to be very accurate, otherwise the pieces won't join together.

2 Using a pencil or ballpoint pen, draw around the template 12 times on different colors of felt or fleece, then cut out the shapes.

▲ Join the sides of the pentagons together.

4 Now join the sides of the pentagons around the central patch together. Can you see that, as you join the sides, the piece starts to stand up and looks like half a ball?

5 Now do the same thing with the other six patches to make the other half of the ball.

▲ Using one pentagon patch as the center, whipstitch pentagon patches to each edge.

3 Wearing a thimble so that you don't hurt your fingers, whipstitch one edge of a pentagon patch to each side of a central pentagon.

Materials

● Tracing paper and cardboard, or template plastic

- - - - - - - - - - - -

● Pencil or ballpoint pen

- - - - - - - - - - - -

● Scraps of felt or fleece, preferably in 12 different colors or patterns

- - - - - - - - - - - -

● Scissors

- - - - - - - - - - - -

● Needle

- - - - - - - - - - - -

● Sewing thread

- - - - - - - - - - - -

● Thimble

- - - - - - - - - - - -

● Batting for stuffing

- - - - - - - - - - - -

3-D and trapunto

Template

use the template at this size or adjust it to make a smaller or larger ball.

Join the two halves, then stuff the ball before sewing up the last patch.

6 Join the two halves together by oversewing the edges; felt doesn't fray, so it's quite easy. Leave the last patch open so that you can fill the ball with batting or Poly-Fil. Stuff the batting or Poly-Fil into the ball, using the end of your pencil or ballpoint pen to push it in. Sew up the final patch and you're ready for a game of catch!

Tips

● You can have the whipstitching showing on the front or, if your sewing isn't very neat and you want to hide it, turn the ball inside out before you stuff it!

● To make a bigger or a smaller ball, alter the size of the pentagon template.

Fancy needle book

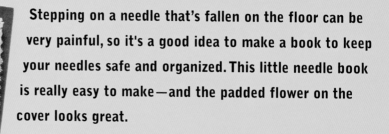

Stepping on a needle that's fallen on the floor can be very painful, so it's a good idea to make a book to keep your needles safe and organized. This little needle book is really easy to make—and the padded flower on the cover looks great.

How to make the needle book

Materials

- Pinking shears
- 4 x 7 inches (18 x 10 cm) brightly colored felt
- Two 4 x 7 inches (18 x 10 cm) pieces of heavy cotton
- Bar soap or white crayon
- Ruler
- Brightly colored embroidery floss
- Needle
- Thimble
- Scraps of colored felt
- Small piece of batting or cotton balls

⚠ Cut the felt and heavy cotton with pinking shears. It looks pretty and won't fray.

1 Using pinking shears, cut one felt and two heavy cotton pieces measuring 4 x 7 inches (10 x 18 cm). (Pinking shears are used for dressmaking to keep seams from fraying and make a cut with a jagged edge. You might have some fancy-edged scissors that you use for craft paper work, and these would work just as well.)

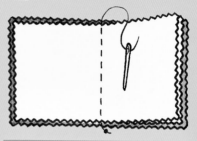

⚠ Stitch along the drawn line using big-stitch quilting stitches and brightly colored thread to join the pieces together.

2 Using bar soap or a white crayon and a ruler, draw a 3½-inch (8.5-cm) line down the middle of the felt and the heavy cotton. Put the two layers of cotton over the felt and sew down the line with bright embroidery floss to join the layers together, finishing with a knot on the inside so that the outside looks nice and neat.

Tip

You can use cotton balls for the stuffing.

⚠ Decorate the front of the book with one of these designs, or make up your own.

⚠ Push batting into the center of the flower and the petals so that they're nicely padded.

5 Add the stalk and leaves, stuffing the leaves as you did the center of the flower—and that's trapunto. It's nice to know you are carrying on a tradition of quilting from 700 years ago!

4 If you decide to use the flower design shown here, cut seven petals and a circle for the center from the felt. Place the circle in the middle of the book cover and sew it down with big-stitch quilting and brightly colored embroidery floss, leaving a ½-inch (1.25-cm) gap. Fluff up some batting until it's puffy, and poke it into the circle with the end of the scissors or a pencil until it makes a nice puffy shape. Now close up the gap with a few more stitches and finish with a knot at the back of the work. Do the same thing with the petals.

3 It really looks like a book, doesn't it? Now you can decorate the cover. Chose a design from the examples in the drawing or make up your own.

Teddy bear and hearts crib hanging

Materials

- Pencil
- Tracing paper
- Paper and fabric scissors
- Pins
- Ballpoint pen
- 4 x 12 inch (10 x 30 cm) piece of red felt
- 9 x 10 inch (23 x 25 cm) piece of yellow felt
- 10 x 14 inch (25 x 36 cm) piece of turquoise felt
- Needle
- Sewing threads to match each color of felt
- Scraps of batting
- Small scraps of black felt
- Black and white embroidery flosses
- 48 inches (122 cm) thin red ribbon

Do you remember when you were younger and you made paper dolls and teddy bears holding hands from folded paper? These teddy bears and hearts have the same feel about them. You can make the hanging to go over a baby's carriage or crib, but it looks just as sweet hanging on a wall from two hooks. The teddy bears' eyes are made of felt—this is safer than buttons, which a baby might swallow.

How to make the crib hanging

▲ Trace the patterns onto paper and cut them out.

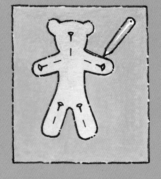

▲ Pin the paper pattern onto felt and draw around it.

1 Using a pencil, trace the patterns for the teddy bear and the heart onto paper and cut them out carefully with paper scissors.

2 Pin the patterns to the felt and draw around them with a ballpoint pen (this is easier than using a pencil, because the pencil catches on the felt). Draw eight hearts on red felt, four teddy bears on yellow felt, and six teddy bears on turquoise felt. Cut out all the shapes.

3 Pin two yellow teddy bears together, with the drawing on the inside in case the ink smudges.

▲ Quilt around the edge, leaving a 1–2-inch (2.5–5-cm) gap.

4 Thread your needle with thread that is the same color as the felt. Start sewing around the edge of the teddy bear with small quilting stitches, leaving a gap of about 1–2 inches (2.5–5 cm).

▲ Stuff the teddy bear with batting.

5 Fluff up some batting and stuff it into the gap, using the blunt end of a pencil to push it in. First stuff the head and arms, then the legs, and finally the tummy.

Templates
shown actual size

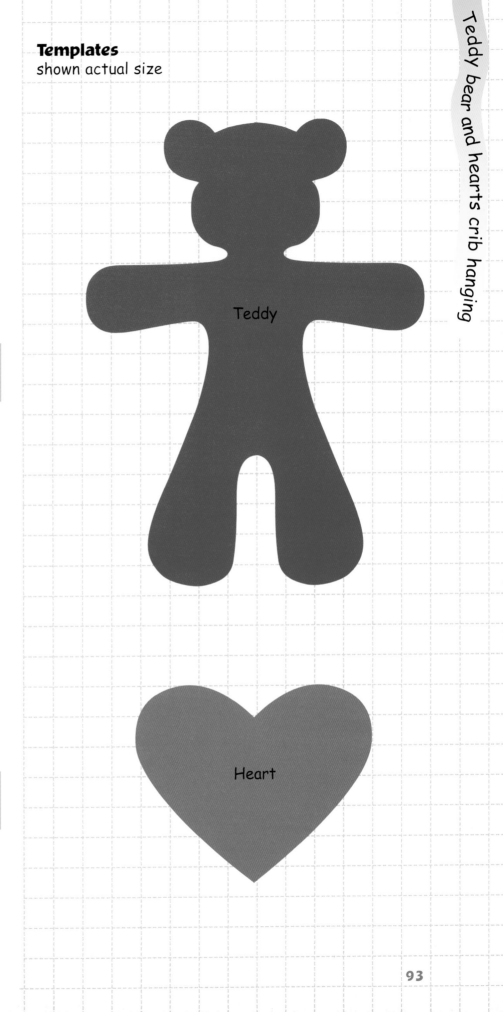

Teddy

Heart

▲ Finish stitching, then bring the needle up through the middle of the teddy bear and cut the thread.

6 Sew up the gap, ending with a backstitch, and then bring the needle through to the front of the teddy bear's tummy and cut off the thread. This is so that you don't get any ugly knots of thread.

7 Make another yellow teddy bear and three turquoise teddy bears in the same way.

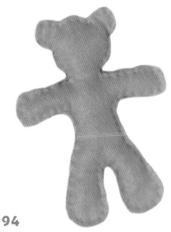

▲ Stitch on the black felt eyes with white embroidery floss.

8 Now add the eyes. Cut little circles of black felt (a good way to cut a really small circle is to use a paper hole puncher). Sew them on, using white embroidery floss. Remember to finish off the thread as you did for quilting the teddy bear.

▲ Embroider the nose and mouth.

9 Stitch on the nose and mouth with small, straight stitches in black thread.

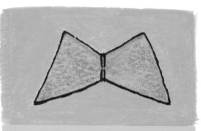

▲ Sew on a red felt bow tie.

10 Complete the teddy bears by adding bow ties made from little bits of leftover red felt.

▲ Make four red felt hearts.

11 Make the hearts in the same way as you made the teddy bears, by stitching together pairs of red felt hearts and stuffing them with batting.

▲ Stitch one heart between each pair of teddy bears.

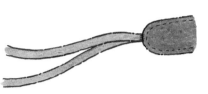

▲ Stitch a ribbon at each end of the row, so that you can hang up the decoration.

Warning

Don't use beads for the eyes because babies may chew the teddies and swallow the beads. Tie the hanging high on the baby carriage so the baby can see it, but can't pull it.

12 Lay out the teddy bears in a row, starting and ending with a turquoise teddy bear. Put one heart between each pair of bears. Join the hearts and teddy bears together by whipstitching the hands to the hearts. Don't they look cute?!

13 Cut the ribbon in half, fold each piece in half to make a loop, and sew one loop to the outer hand of the teddy bear at each end of the row. Tie each ribbon to the baby's crib or carriage.

Something for nothing

"Make do and mend" is a popular saying that you might have heard—and it's well suited to quilting. This section shows you how to make those tiny leftover scraps of fabric and batting into something useful.

This is carrying on an old tradition in quilting. In the old days, people used to cut up their old clothes and make them into bed quilts. So in this section, there are projects that use clothes that you've outgrown to make a really useful hanging and great fabric pictures. You can also transform plain white cotton into your own designer fabric with crayons and leaves, and even print fabric with flowers and leaves that you've picked up for free in the park or in your backyard.

Collecting things to recycle

It's a lot of fun to collect things to recycle and make into a quilted project. Your friends and relatives will start giving you all their reusable fabrics when they know you are a quilter. You'll be amazed at the number of treasures that will arrive on your doorstep!

When you have bits of fabric left over from your sewing projects, sort them into different colors and put them in clear plastic bags, so that when you want to use them, you can see at a glance what you have got. It's amazing what you can make out of tiny bits that would have been thrown into the garbage can! This is a job you can ask a young sister or brother to help with.

THREADS

Threads can also be stored in plastic bags, but if you are now an enthusiastic stitcher, you may have a needlework basket to keep all your threads and needles organized.

OLD CLOTHES AND HOME FURNISHINGS

When you're using outgrown clothes for the projects, make sure you ask for permission before you cut them up! You can buy very inexpensive old clothes at garage sales and thrift stores. Look at summer dresses that you've outgrown: there might be some nice pictures on the fabric, which you could fussy cut and bond onto one of your projects, as we did in Seashore Scenes (Project 3).

Household items can be recycled, too—with your parents' permission, of course. Old bedsheets that have worn out in the center can be used as background fabric for projects such as the Leaf-Print Cushion (Project 18) or the Fantastic Flower Basket (Project 21). Or maybe your family has moved and there are some curtains and pillow covers that you don't use any more?

You can also use old clothes as stuffing: panty hose and socks, for example, can be cut into shreds and used instead of batting for stuffing 3-D projects.

Always wash old clothes and home furnishings before you cut them up.

BATTING

You will have lots of scraps of batting left from the quilting projects, which you can use to stuff the Teddy Bear and Hearts Hanging (Project 17) and for the trapunto techniques. Pull the batting apart as described in trapunto techniques (see page 82).

BUTTONS

People have been recycling buttons for years, and most adults remember a button tin from their childhood. Even if the fabric is too badly worn for you to be able to reuse it, you can get a lot of buttons from just one shirt: not only are there buttons down the front and on both sleeves and collar, but there are also spare ones sewn inside the seam.

Buttons can be used purely for decoration, like the flowers in the house picture or as eyes for animals or birds. They can also be used instead of quilting to hold the three layers of the sandwich together.

Leaf-print cushion

Did you know that all plants and leaves contain natural dyes, and that in the olden days this was the only way to dye cloth for clothes? This project involves hammering leaves and flowers onto fabric, so that the dyes come out and make a print. It's fun to do, but it's kind of noisy, so tell the people in your house what you're up to.

You will get different colors from leaves and flowers, depending on the season of the year. Spring and early summer are the best times, as the sap is rising in the plants. To release the natural dyes that are in the plants and make them stick to the fabric, the fabric has to be soaked in alum. You can buy alum from pharmacies or from craft stores. The other chemical that you need is washing soda, which fixes the color to the fabric so that it doesn't wash out.

Materials

- White cotton fabric that has been previously washed
- Water
- Plastic bucket
- 2 oz (50 g) alum
- 1 dessertspoon plus 1 teaspoon of washing soda
- Flowers and leaves
- Adhesive tape
- Old newspapers
- Hammer

- Paper towel
- Rubber band
- Blunt kitchen knife
- Flat dish or cat litter box
- Plastic food wrap
- Fusible bonding web
- Iron
- Pale blue fabric
- Paper
- Pencil

- Scissors
- 14 inches (35 cm) white fabric for the cushion back
- White quilting thread
- Needle
- Thimble
- Fabric backing for cushion, as in Project 6, Quilted Picture Cushion, page 46

How to make the leaf-print cushion

1 Ask an adult to prepare the fabric for you. For 1 yard (1 meter) of cloth, put 1 pint (0.5 liter) of hot water in a plastic bucket, and dissolve 2 ounces (50 g) of alum in it.

▲ Wait for the hot water and alum mixture to cool down, then add washing soda and cold water.

2 When the mixture has cooled, add a dessertspoonful of washing soda. The mixture will bubble up, but don't be alarmed at this. Add enough cold water to make the mixture up to 8 pints (4 liters) and soak the fabric for 8 hours or overnight.

3 Discard the alum mixture and dry the fabric naturally. You now have enough fabric to use for many projects, and the treated fabric will keep indefinitely.

4 Pick some flowers and leaves; you will have to experiment with different plants to see which work the best. Try to choose different shapes of leaves.

What is Alum?

Alum is the common name for aluminum sulfate. It was used long ago, by the early Egyptians, as a fixing agent when dyeing fabrics and in water purification.

▲ Stick the leaves and flowers to the white fabric with adhesive tape, vein side down.

5 Place the flowers and leaves on the treated fabric, with the vein next to the fabric, and stick them down with adhesive tape. Lay the fabric on a pad of newspapers on the ground or on a very sturdy table.

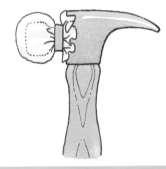

▲ Cover the head of a hammer with a paper towel, using a rubber band to hold the towel in place.

6 Cover the ball of the hammer with some paper towel and secure it with a rubber band.

▲ Put the fabric on a thick wad of old newspapers, and hit the flowers and leaves with the hammer to release the dyes.

7 Hit the fabric with the hammer until the dye and the image begin to appear.

8 Take off the tape and scrape away the crushed remains of the leaf with a blunt knife. You've made a print! Let it dry naturally.

9 To fix the image, dissolve a teaspoonful of washing soda in a little hot water, add this to 4 pints (2 liters) of cold water, and soak your fabric in it for at least 6 hours in a flat dish or cat litter box covered with plastic food wrap.

10 Wash the fabric in soapy water to remove any bits of leaf that remain. Leave the fabric to dry. The image is now fixed—but don't leave it in very strong sunlight, or it will fade.

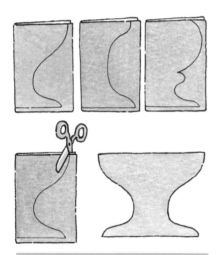

▲ Draw half a vase shape on folded paper, and cut it out.

11 To make the vase, iron 6 inches (15 cm) of fusible bonding web to the back of pale blue fabric (or ask an adult to help). Make a vase pattern, by folding a piece of paper in half and drawing half a vase shape, or tracing the template, and cutting it out. Try different shapes and sizes until you get one you really like.

12 Draw around your paper pattern on the wrong side of the blue fabric, and cut out the shape. Remove the paper backing, and iron the vase shape onto a 16-inch (40-cm) square of white fabric (or ask an adult to do this for you).

Template
shown actual size

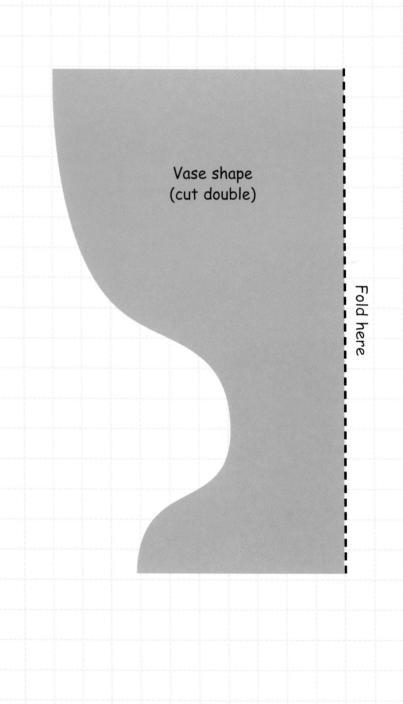

Vase shape
(cut double)

Fold here

▲ Arrange the flowers and leaves in and around the vase.

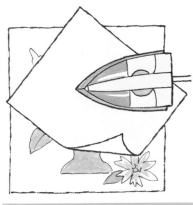

▲ Once you have the picture you want, iron the shapes onto the fabric.

14 Place the flower and leaf shapes in the vase and move them around until you've got a picture that you like. To make it more interesting, put some flower heads next to the vase, so that they look as if they have fallen out.

15 Remove the paper backing from the shapes, place them in position, and cover with a damp cloth. Iron to fix them in place.

16 You can now make your very special picture into a cushion following the instructions for Project 6, Quilted Picture Cushion, pages 46–49.

▲ Roughly cut out the nicest flower and leaf prints.

13 Now select your best flower and leaf prints. Iron fusible bonding web onto the back of the fabric (you might want to get an adult to help you with this), and cut out the shapes. Because the flowers and leaves are on a white background fabric, you can cut them out very roughly and the edges won't show.

101

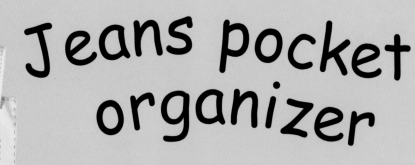

Jeans pocket organizer

Something for nothing

I'm sure you have jeans that you've outgrown just sitting in the closet. At last you have a use for them! Cut off the back pockets, stitch them onto a bright backing with nice big stitches—and you've got somewhere to store your treasures and keep your room looking neat. Some jeans pockets have flaps with Velcro, so you can keep things safe from prying eyes. The size of this quilt will depend on how many jeans pockets you have; you can always ask your brothers and sisters or friends for theirs or buy them from thrift stores.

Materials

- Large piece of solid-colored fabric for the front of the quilt

- Backing fabric 2 inches (5 cm) smaller than the front of the quilt

- Batting the same size as the backing fabric

- Safety pins

- 6 jeans pockets

- Fabric scissors

- Light-colored crayon or bar soap

- Ruler

- Pinking shears

- Red or brightly colored sewing thread

- Needle

- Thimble

- Pencil

- Three 5 x 12 inch (13 x 30 cm) strips of the same colored fabric as the front

- Three brightly colored buttons

How to make the pocket organizer

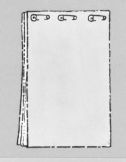

▲ Make a "sandwich," with the batting in the middle, and safety-pin or baste the layers together.

1 Place the backing fabric right side down, with the batting on top, and the front fabric of the organizer right side up on top of the batting. Make sure the front fabric covers the batting and backing, leaving 1 inch (2.5 cm) extra all around. Safety-pin or baste to hold the three layers together.

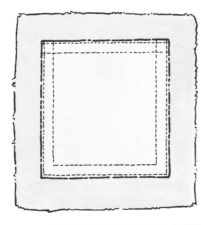

▲ Cut the pockets off the jeans, leaving about 2 inches (5 cm) of fabric around the edges.

2 Cut out the jeans pockets, leaving about 2 inches (5 cm) all around the edges.

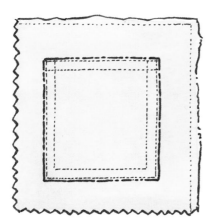

▲ Draw a line about 1 inch (2.5 cm) beyond the edges of the pockets, and then cut along this line with pinking shears.

3 Using a light-colored crayon or bar soap and a ruler, draw a line 1½ inches (4 cm) from the stitching of the pocket and cut along this line with the pinking shears. This makes a nice jagged edge, which won't fray.

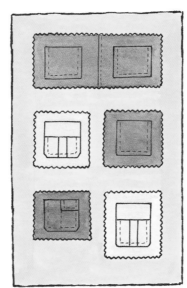

▲ Arrange the pockets on the background fabric.

4 Place the pockets on the front of the organizer, and move them around until you like the arrangement. If you put two pockets side by side, it looks good if their tops are in line.

5 Pin the pockets onto the organizer with safety pins, so that you won't prick yourself when you're sewing them.

6 Thread your needle with bright-colored thread. I used a thicker thread than normal, but you can use ordinary sewing thread used double.

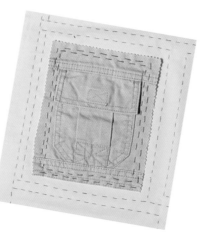

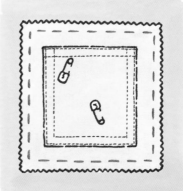

▲ Pin the pockets to the background fabric, and make big quilting stitches in brightly-colored thread to stitch them in place.

7 Put a thimble on your middle finger to protect it while you quilt. Stitch around the pocket about ¼ inch (0.6 cm) from the edge, using large stitches. This is called "big-stitch quilting"—it's much quicker to do than the small quilting stitches you've used in other projects!

▲ Now stitch a second row of stitches around the pockets.

8 When you've sewn all the pockets, take out the safety pins and add another row of stitching inside the one you've just done. It looks really great if the stitches don't line up exactly with the ones in the first row, because it makes a nice pattern.

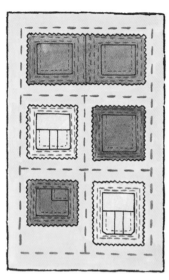

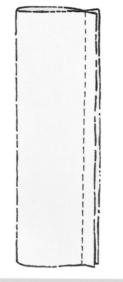

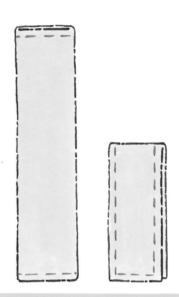

▲ More colorful stitching between the pockets makes the organizer look bright and cheerful.

▲ Fold the tab fabric in half, right sides together, and stitch along the long edge to make a tube.

▲ Turn under the raw edges, and stitch in place.

9 Now draw some lines around your pockets with a sharp pencil and ruler and do some more big stitching along the lines. It looks very effective, doesn't it?

11 Make some tabs so that you can hang the organizer on your wall. Take three 5 x 12 inch (13 x 30 cm) strips of the same fabric you used for the front of the organizer. Fold each strip in half lengthwise, right sides together, and either machine- or hand-stitch ¼ inch (0.6 cm) from the edge.

13 Turn under ¼ inch (0.6 cm) at each end of each strip, and sew all around the edges with big stitches in bright-colored thread.

▲ At the top of the organizer, fold fabric over to the back, and stitch it down with big quilting stitches.

10 To cover the raw edges, turn the 1 inch (2.5 cm) of extra fabric from the front of the organizer over to the back and stitch it down, using big stitches just as you did to sew on the pockets.

▲ Turn the tube right side out.

12 Turn each strip the right way out. (This is a little bit tricky, but you can poke your ruler into the tube to help you.)

▲ Sew the tabs to the top of the organizer by stitching a big button to the front.

14 Fold each tab in half lengthwise, and place them on the top of the quilt—one end should be on the front of the quilt, and the other end on the back. Stitch a big button to the tab that's on the front of the quilt and stitch through all layers of fabric to fix the tabs in place. Make sure you sew the button on very securely.

Something for nothing

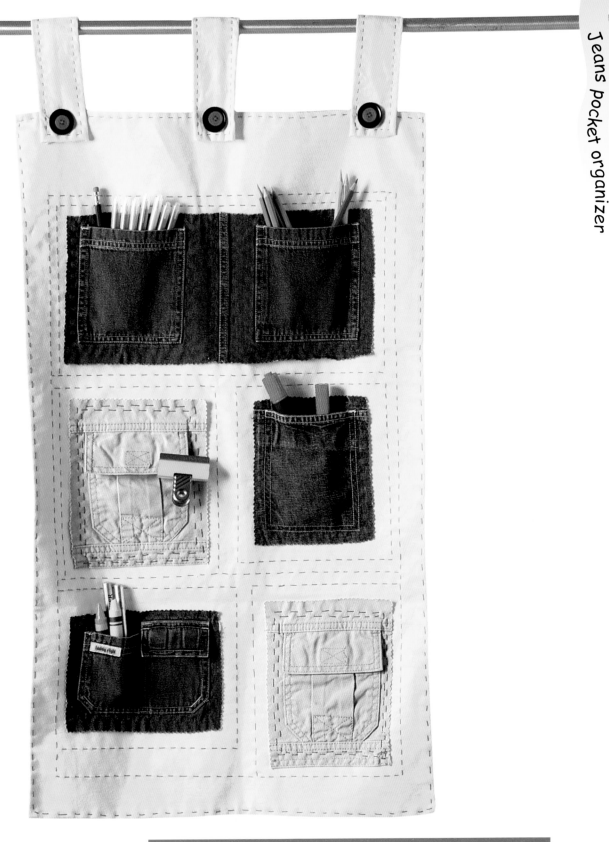

15 Ask an adult to put some hooks on the wall, find a stick to thread through the loops, and there you have a great-looking quilt that is really useful.

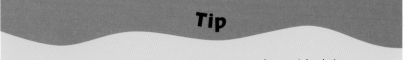

Tip

If you can't find a big red button, sew a large black button on first, and then sew a smaller red button on top.

105

Quilted house

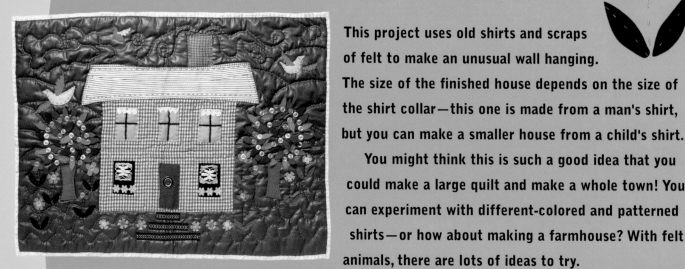

This project uses old shirts and scraps of felt to make an unusual wall hanging. The size of the finished house depends on the size of the shirt collar—this one is made from a man's shirt, but you can make a smaller house from a child's shirt.

You might think this is such a good idea that you could make a large quilt and make a whole town! You can experiment with different-colored and patterned shirts—or how about making a farmhouse? With felt animals, there are lots of ideas to try.

This project uses up little pieces of felt or fleece that you have left over from other projects, such as the snuggle rug, the pentagon ball, or the needle book. It's always nice to use up scraps, because that's what patchwork and quilting are all about. The list of materials might seem very long for a recycled project, but you will already have a lot of them in your scrap bag.

Materials

- 22½ x 30½ inches (57 x 77 cm) backing fabric
- 21 x 29 inches (53 x 74 cm) batting
- 21 x 29 inches (53 x 74 cm) green fabric for the background
- Safety pins
- Striped or checkered shirt collar for the roof
- Scissors
- Red-checkered shirt for the house

- Pins
- Sewing needle and large-eyed needle
- Red, blue, green, and black embroidery floss
- Green, gray, and blue sewing threads
- Small piece of checkered shirt for the chimney
- 6 x 6 inches (15 x 15 cm) yellow or black/dark blue felt for windows
- 2 x 4 inches (5 x 10 cm) colored felt for door

- Thin black ribbon, scraps of lace, or flower-shaped trimmings to decorate the windows
- Large, gold-colored button for door knocker
- Scraps of felt in green, yellow, orange, pink, and blue for the leaves and flowers
- About 50 small shirt buttons for flowers and tree
- 12 inches (30 cm) colored ribbon for the steps
- Bar soap or white crayon

How to make the quilted house

1 Make a "sandwich" by placing the backing fabric right side down on the table, with the batting centered on top of it, and the green background fabric on top of the batting. About 1½ inches (4 cm) of the backing fabric should be showing at the edge all the way around. Smooth out the layers with your hands, then pin with safety pins to hold the layers together.

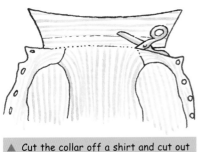

▲ Cut the collar off a shirt and cut out the label.

2 Cut the collar off the shirt (if the neck is worn, turn the collar over and use the back), and cut out the label.

3 From a checkered shirt, cut an oblong for the house measuring 10 x 12 inches (25 x 30 cm).

Note

If you're using a small shirt collar, you will need to make the sizes of all the other things smaller.

▲ Using big-stitch quilting and red embroidery floss, stitch the oblong to the green background.

4 Place the oblong in the middle of the green backing fabric, about 4 inches (10 cm) from the bottom border. Pin and turn under ¼ inch (0.6 cm) along the base and sides, and quilt down with big-stitch quilting, using a large-eyed needle threaded with red embroidery floss.

▲ Blanket-stitch the roof to the top of the house, using brightly colored thread.

5 Place the collar on the top of the house to make the roof, and pin it in place. Blanket-stitch it in place, using brightly colored embroidery floss in a contrasting color.

6 Quilt all around the roof, using the embroidery floss, about 1 inch (2.5 cm) from the edge. Some collars have stiffeners inside them, which makes it difficult to stitch through them; if your collar is like this, don't worry about quilting: the roof will look just fine with the blanket stitch holding it on.

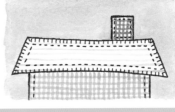

▲ Quilt all around the roof about 1 inch (2.5 cm) from the edge.

7 From a checkered shirt in a different color, cut a chimney measuring 2½ x 3 inches (6 x 8 cm). Pin it in place, and quilt it down, once again using a bright- and contrasting-colored embroidery floss.

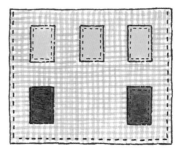

▲ Quilt the windows to the house. You can use different colors to make it look as if the lights are on, or off.

8 Now add the windows: you can choose if you want the lights to be on or off. If you want the windows to be lit up, use yellow felt; if you want them to be dark, use black or dark blue felt. Cut five windows measuring 2 x 3 inches (5 x 8 cm), and arrange three on the second floor and two on the first. Quilt them down around the edges using brightly colored, contrasting embroidery floss. The felt doesn't fray, so there's no need to turn under the edge of the fabric.

107

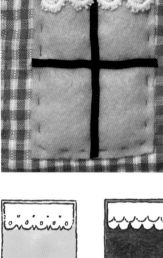

Stick lace to the top.

Add a flower-shaped trim to look like a window box.

Stitch thin ribbon to look like windowpanes.

Sew strips of fabric to the sides to look like curtains.

▲ Here are some ideas for decorating the windows.

9 Add curtains at the windows—look at the drawing to get some ideas. You could stitch a small piece of lace at the top or along the side, or maybe add window-box flowers made from flower-shaped decorative trim. Narrow ribbon stitched over the windows makes windowpanes.

▲ Quilt around the edge of the door and sew on a button for the door knocker.

10 Cut a 2 x 4 inch (5 x 10 cm) piece of brightly colored felt for the front door and quilt it down using a bright-colored embroidery floss. Add a gold-colored button to make a nice and shiny door knocker.

▲ Quilt around the edge of the tree trunks, and cut leaf shapes from felt.

11 Now your house needs a yard. To make the trees, cut two tree trunks from leftover scraps of felt or fleece. Quilt the trunks to the sides of the house. Cut some leaf shapes, too— if you don't want to use felt again, you could make your leaves from leftovers from Project 18 (the Leaf-Print Cushion). It's your yard—you decide.

▲ Stitch a small button to one end of each leaf to hold it in place.

12 Sew the leaves onto the trunks by sewing a small button on one end—this will make them stick up and look realistic.

▲ Cut flower shapes from felt, and stitch a small button to the centers to fix them in place.

13 Now make flowers in different colors of felt. Cut some circles of felt and cut triangular notches out of the sides to make petal shapes—or cut squares and round off the corners. Stitch them down with buttons.

▲ Make "steps" leading up to the front door from strips of narrow ribbon.

14 Make some steps leading up to the front door by quilting down some strips of narrow ribbon with brightly colored embroidery floss.

15 Using bar soap or a white crayon, draw some wavy lines in the yard, below the house, and quilt along the lines with a bright green embroidery floss.

▲ Stitch lines to represent the hills, clouds, and smoke.

16 Draw some hills and clouds as above and quilt them with bright-colored embroidery floss.

17 Draw swirls and curves of smoke coming from the chimney and quilt the lines in black embroidery floss.

▲ Cut bird shapes from felt and quilt them to the picture, adding a few stitches for an eye.

18 Some birds in the sky or the trees will complete the picture. Cut the shapes from felt or from the bonded cleaning cloths used in Project 21 (Fantastic Flower Basket). Quilt them down with a bright-colored embroidery floss.

19 To finish off the edges, turn under a hem on the backing fabric, and fold the backing fabric over to the front of the picture. Pin it to the green fabric and quilt it down, using a brightly colored embroidery floss. We did this in Project 3 (Seashore Scenes Quilt) and in Project 8 (Circle Quilt for Teddy Bear).

109

Fantastic flower basket

This would make a great picture to hang in the kitchen or give as a present. It's a really cheap and cheerful project, because it's made from bonded cleaning cloths. You can buy them from any supermarket or general store, and they are very inexpensive. They don't fray, which makes them very easy to use. The thicker felt-type ones look really good and are a fraction of the price of real felt.

Materials

- Open-weave cleaning cloth for the basket
- Scissors
- 14 x 14 inches (35 x 35 cm) background fabric (we used red, but you can use any color)
- Needle
- Yellow and green thread
- Thread the same color as the basket
- Thimble

- 15 x 15 inches (38 x 38 cm) backing fabric
- 14 x 14 inches (35 x 35 cm) batting
- Safety pin
- Cleaning cloths in various colors, including green
- Assorted buttons
- Bar soap or white crayon

How to make the flower basket

▲ Quilt the basket shape to the background fabric.

1 Cut out a basket shape from the open-weave cloth and place it in the center of your chosen background fabric. Using brightly-colored thread, quilt around the edge. Add some lines of quilting in a thread the same color as the basket.

Templates
shown actual size

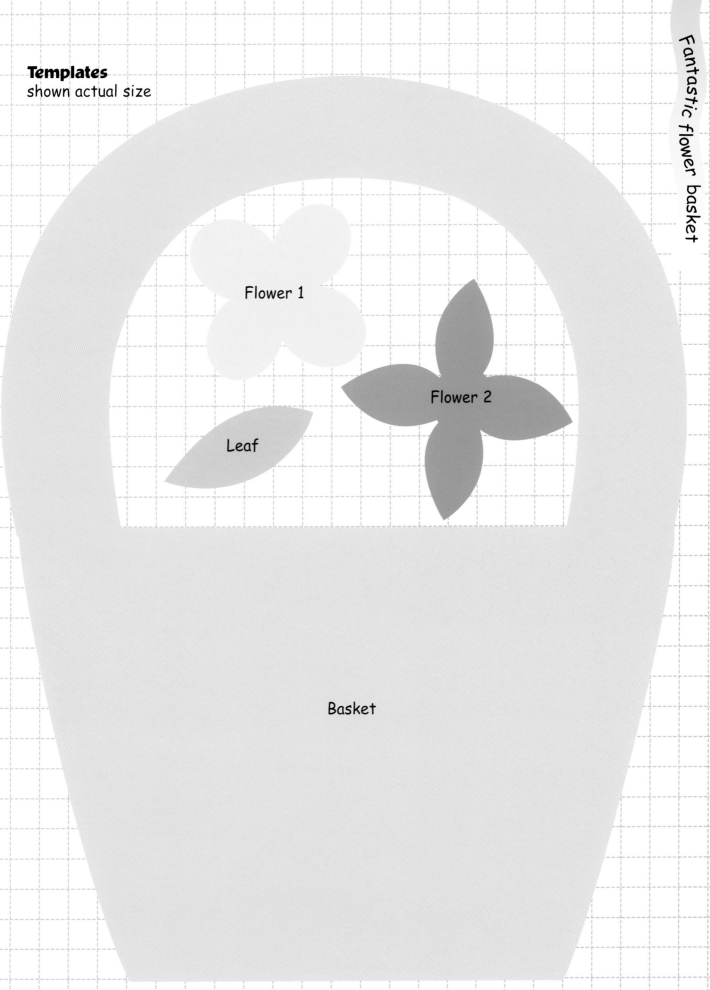

Flower 1

Flower 2

Leaf

Basket

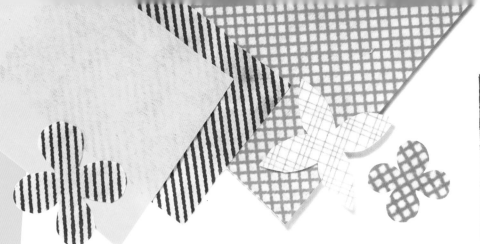

▲ Quilt around the outer edge of the picture in green thread, using big-stitch quilting.

2 Make a "sandwich" again! Place the backing fabric right side down, with the batting centered on top of it and the background fabric (with the basket) right side up on top of the batting. The backing will stick out all around the edges because it's 1 inch (2.5 cm) larger than the top layer. Safety-pin the layers together.

4 Arrange the flowers in the basket. It looks better if some are outside the basket handle and if some have fallen out of the basket completely. Sew them in place with a button from the button box or from old clothes, using yellow thread. You might even be lucky enough to find some flower-shaped buttons.

6 Draw around the basket and flower shapes with hard soap or a white crayon about ½ inch (1.25 cm) from the edges. Quilt along the line with big-stitch quilting in a green thread.

▲ Cut green leaves and stitch them in place with green thread.

▲ Cut out flower shapes in different colors and stitch them in place by stitching a button in the center.

5 Cut some leaf shapes in different sizes from green cleaning cloths and quilt them in place, using green thread.

3 Cut flowers from the cleaning cloths, just as you did for the Quilted House project on page 108. If you like, you can make these flowers a little more exotic by adding a double layer of petals.

Fold the backing fabric over to the front and quilt down with big-stitch quilting to make a neat border.

7 Turn under a hem all around the edge, fold the backing fabric over to the front of the picture, and quilt it down with big-stitch quilting.

Ready-threaded needle case

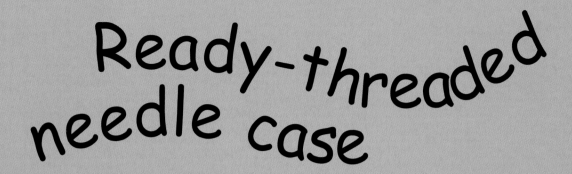

This is a really clever little needle case, as your needles are threaded and ready for use! It would make a lovely present for someone who does not have very good eyesight. The pieces of felt and batting are so small that you can use up scraps left over from other projects.

Materials

- Tracing paper
- Pencil
- Glue
- Cardboard
- Paper scissors
- Ballpoint pen
- 5 x 11 inches (13 x 28 cm) yellow felt
- 5 x 11 inches (13 x 28 cm) blue felt
- 2 x 8 inches (5 x 20 cm) batting

- Fabric scissors
- Pins
- Needle
- Thick, brightly colored thread
- 3 buttons
- Snap
- Spool of quilting thread
- Packet of needles

How to make the needle case

1 Trace templates 1 and 2, stick the tracing onto the cardboard, and cut out the template with paper scissors.

2 Using a ballpoint pen, draw around template 1 three times—once on blue felt, once on yellow felt, and once on batting. Cut out the pieces.

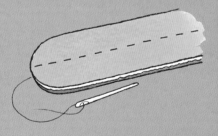

⚠ Stitch the layers together with big-stitch quilting.

3 Sandwich the batting between the two pieces of felt, pin the layers together, and do a line of big-stitch quilting along the middle with thick, brightly colored thread.

Templates
shown actual size

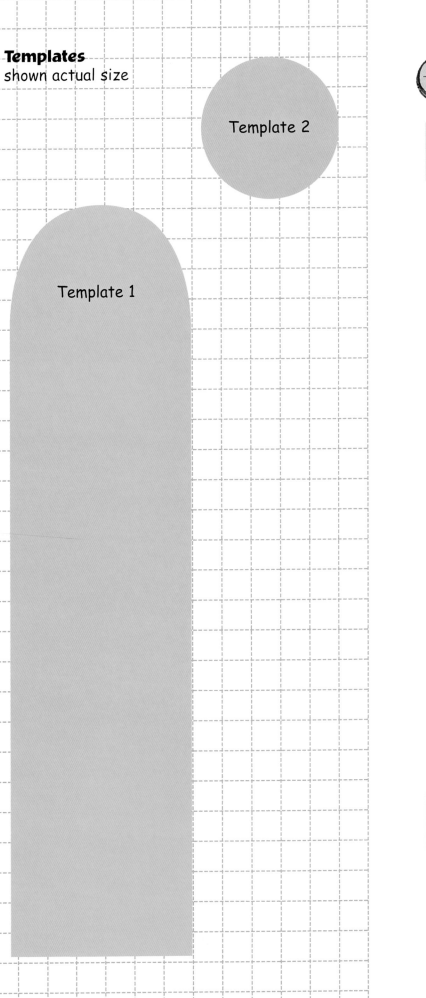

Template 2

Template 1

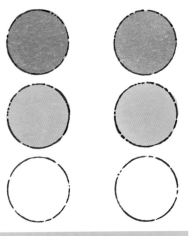

△ Blanket-stitch around the edge.

4 Now blanket-stitch all around the edge—do you remember this stitch from the Handy Snuggle Rug, page 63?

△ Cut two blue, two yellow, and two cardboard pieces from template 2.

5 Using a ballpoint pen, draw around template 2 and cut out two pieces of yellow felt, two pieces of blue felt, and two pieces of cardboard.

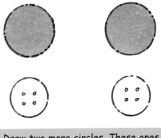

△ Draw two more circles. These ones are smaller than the template, but larger than your buttons.

6 On blue felt, draw two small circles slightly larger than your buttons and cut them out—you can either draw the circles freehand or draw around a coin.

115

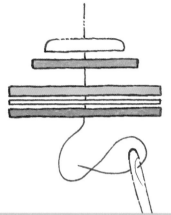

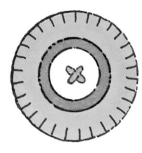

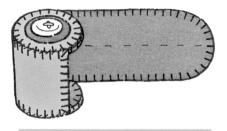

△ Take the needle and thread through the holes in the button and then through all the different layers to hold them together.

△ Blanket-stitch around the edge.

△ Whipstitch the circular piece to the felt rectangle, leaving a 2-inch (5-cm) gap.

7 Now it's time to make another kind of sandwich! Stack one large blue felt circle, one cardboard circle, one yellow felt circle, one small blue circle, and one button on top of each other. Sew on the button, stitching through all the other layers so that the sandwich is held together.

8 Now blanket-stitch around the edge. Make another "sandwich" exactly the same.

9 Whipstitch one of these sandwiches to the felt-and-batting piece that you made in step 3, leaving a gap of 2 inches (5 cm).

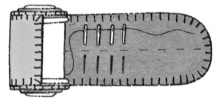

△ Thread each needle, one after the other, without cutting the thread, and insert each needle into the felt when you've finished.

10 Do the same with the other sandwich. You have now made a little container for the quilting thread. Slot the spool of quilting thread into the container, and start threading the needles: thread one, insert the needle into the felt near the container, pull the thread a little farther, and thread the next needle. Continue until you have threaded eight to ten needles. When you're ready to sew, take out the last needle in the felt and pull through as much thread as you need—the next needle in line is threaded and ready for use! Clever, isn't it?

Tip

You can make different-sized cases by drawing around the top of your thread spools and making them fatter or thinner—you could even make a double-decker one for holding two spools at a time!

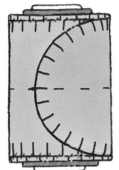

△ Roll up the felt strip with the spool of thread inside, and make a mark to show you where to stitch on the snap.

△ Stitch a button to the outside of the roll to cover up the stitches where you sewed on the snap.

11 To make a neat fastening, roll up the felt strip with the spool of thread inside, and make a mark with a ballpoint pen where the strip ends.

12 Sew half the snap on the mark and the other half on the inside of the end of the felt strip. Because you'll probably be able to see the stitches on the front of the needle case, sew a button on top to disguise them.

Rubbed-leaf cushion

Rubbing is a way of transferring a pattern from something that has a rough texture onto paper. You may have heard of brass rubbing: this is when people put paper over brass plates in churches and lightly rub the surface with wax, so that the pattern of the brass comes through onto the paper. You may have done the same thing with coins to make toy money for playing store when you were younger.

In this project, we're rubbing leaves with fabric crayons to make our own fabric for a great colored cushion. Be as inventive as you like: leaves don't have to be green or even the colors that you see in the fall. You could try pink, blue, or yellow and invent some new species.

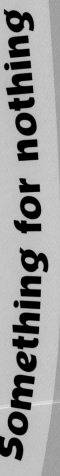

Materials

- Leaves of various shapes
- Fabric crayons in different colors
- White cotton fabric or calico
- Paper towel
- Iron
- Fusible bonding web
- Scissors
- 14 x 14 inches (35 x 35 cm) fabric for the background

- 14 x 14 inches (35 x 35 cm) backing fabric
- 14 x 14 inches (35 x 35 cm) batting
- Safety pins
- Quilting needle
- Green thread for quilting
- Thimble
- Fabric to make cushion back

Something for nothing

How to make the rubbed-leaf cushion

crayon
fabric
leaf

▲ Choose leaves that have raised veins—and look for different sizes and shapes.

1 Pick some leaves that have raised veins. Use different shapes of leaf to make the project interesting.

▲ Rub the side of the crayon over the fabric: the leaf pattern will soon start to show through.

5 You will need about 25 leaves for the cushion front. When you have enough, put some paper towel over the leaf prints and iron with a hot iron to fix the crayons. (You might want to ask an adult to help with this.) When the prints have been ironed, the colors won't rub off and the fabric can be washed as usual.

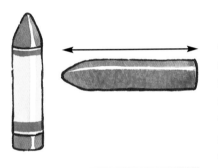

▲ Peel off the paper so that you can use the sides of the crayons.

2 Peel off the paper that covers the fabric crayons, because we are going to use the sides of the crayons, not the tips.

3 Place a leaf on a table or flat surface, put the white fabric on top of it, and rub the fabric crayon lightly over the leaf, using the side rather than the tip, as this allows you to cover a large area quickly. The shape and the veins of the leaf will come through onto the fabric. Magic, isn't it? Don't worry if the edges look a little messy: we're going to cut each leaf out to make a nice, clean edge.

4 Continue making leaf rubbings, using different-shaped leaves and different-colored crayons. You could even try using two colors on some leaves; it looks really pretty.

▲ Iron fusible bonding web onto the leaf and cut out each shape as neatly as you can.

6 Iron some fusible bonding web onto the back of the leaf fabric and cut out each individual leaf. By doing this, you can cut out the messy bits around the edges.

119

△ Decide where you want the leaf prints to go. You could make a picture of a bunch of leaves and draw on the stems with a fabric crayon, or just scatter them to make a pretty pattern.

7 Peel the paper off the back of the leaves and place them on the cushion front. It's up to you how you arrange them. Look at the drawings for some ideas: you might want to make a bunch of leaves, or just a pretty pattern. Move the leaves around until you get an arrangement that you like—and remember to vary the shapes and colors.

8 Place a damp cloth on top of the leaves and iron with a warm iron to fuse the leaves to the front fabric. Again, you might want to ask an adult to help you with this. You now have your very own homemade fabric.

Tip

If you don't want to use leaves, you could use other textures, such as lace, for making rubbings.

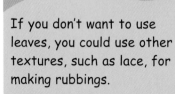

batting — leaf fabric ————
back ————

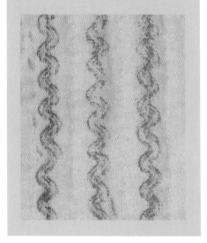

△ Pin the layers together with safety pins.

9 Now for the quilting. Put the backing fabric right side down on the table, with the batting on top of it, and the leaf fabric right side up on top of the batting. Pin with safety pins to hold all the layers together.

▲ Quilt around the outside of each leaf, using green thread.

10 Starting in the middle and working toward the edge, quilt around the outside of the leaf shapes with green thread. Remember to keep looking at the back to make sure you don't have any creases. Actually this really doesn't matter; it won't show, because it will be inside the cushion, but it's good practice to check on the back as you work.

11 Make your quilted fabric into a cushion, as described in Project 6, Quilted Picture Cushion, on pages 46–49.

12 Sit back and admire your handiwork. Next time you go for a walk, you'll be able to think of a use for all those beautiful fallen leaves!

121

What went wrong?

We all make mistakes, and when we're learning a new skill, some things are bound to go wrong. Don't panic and give up—if there's no one in your family who can help, maybe someone at school will lend a helping hand. If you read the instructions for each project carefully, you shouldn't have any trouble, but here are a few common problems and their solutions.

☹ My seams are falling apart

☺ If you're sewing by hand, did you secure the thread with a good knot? If your knots keep coming undone, try using a backstitch or two to start the seam.

☺ Are you pulling the stitches tight enough? The two pieces should be tightly stuck together.

☺ If you're sewing by machine, did you start by making a backstitch?

☺ If you can pull the seam, is the tension on the stitch correct? Get an adult to help you fix the tension and always remember to practice the stitch on a spare piece of fabric before you start sewing the "real" piece of work.

☹ When I try to draw the lines on the fabric, it slips

☺ Try putting another larger piece of fabric on the table, then put the fabric you are marking on top of this. This will keep the top fabric from sliding around on the slippery table.

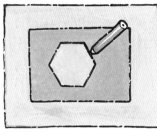

☺ Another method is to put the fabric that you want to mark on top of a piece of fine sandpaper from the hardware store.

☹ I keep pricking my finger with the needle

☺ Wear a thimble or even two thimbles—one on the third finger of your right hand (or your left hand if you're left handed) and one on the index

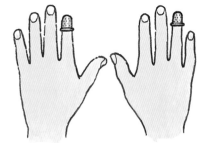

finger of the other hand. If you don't have a thimble or can't find one the right size, put adhesive tape or masking tape around your finger.

☺ If you do prick your finger and get blood on your work, spit on a piece of fabric and wipe it over the bloodstain. The mark will soon come off.

☹ My quilting stitches are uneven

☺ This is just a matter of practice. Don't panic—after a day or two, you will be getting them nice and even.

☹ My quilting stitches are too large

☺ Try using a smaller needle. Again, smaller stitches will come with practice.

☹ My seams are wobbly

☺ Did you draw a line on the fabric to guide your sewing? Are you sewing on that line?

☹ I can't thread my needle

☺ Get a needle threader from the sewing store or persuade a brother or sister to thread your needles for you.

☺ Use the Ready-Threaded Needle Case (Project 22)—then you have to thread your needles only occasionally.

☹ My thread gets tangled up

☺ Use a shorter thread: it saves time in the long run.

☺ Pull your thread through some beeswax or over a candle, as this makes it less likely to tangle. Or use quilting thread, which is slightly waxed and doesn't tangle so much.

☹ My scissors won't cut

☺ Are you sure you have two pairs—one for paper and one for fabric? Paper will blunt scissors. Tie a piece of fabric on your fabric scissors, so that you know which pair is which, and hide them from the rest of the family!

☺ You can buy a scissor sharpener from the fabric store. Or, you can have them professionally sharpened at most sewing stores.

☹ The color comes out of my fabric when it's ironed

☺ Did you wash it before you started work? It's always a good idea to wash fabric before you use it in case the color runs.

☹ My fabric has melted!

☺ Was the iron too hot? Always be sure the iron is set to the right temperature for the type of fabric you're using.

☹ My templates are sliding around

☺ Attach some felt or sandpaper to the back of the template. It will grip the fabric better.

☹ My fabric crayons are smudging

☺ Fabric crayons are very sticky, so if you are using them for rubbings (as in Project 23), it is better to take the wrapping paper from them and break them in half, then use them on their sides. This way, you will get a better print and won't get sticky smudges. Iron each rubbing as you do it, putting paper on top so as not to dirty the iron.

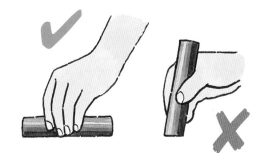

☺ If you are drawing a picture, put some paper over the part you have drawn so that your hand doesn't smudge what you have just drawn. Or iron the drawing a few times before you have finished it.

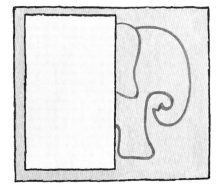

Glossary

APPLIQUÉ
Stitching one piece of fabric on top of another.

BACKING FABRIC
A piece of fabric used for the back of the quilt or cushion.

BACKSTITCH
A stitch where the needle goes back to the previous stitch to make a continuous line of stitching.

BASTING STITCH
A long running stitch used to hold fabric in place before hand- or machine-stitching.

BATTING
A fluffy fabric made from cotton or synthetic fibers. It is used to make a padded, warm layer.

BIAS BINDING
A narrow strip of fabric cut on the diagonal grain of the fabric and used for binding edges and curved edges.

CHANNEL
A strip of fabric sewn to the top of a bag to thread a ribbon for pulling the bag top together.

CONTOUR QUILTING
Quilting in lines echoing a shape, as in lines on a map.

CRAZY QUILT
A quilt made from random shapes and sizes of fabrics. Silks, satins, and velvets are often used, and the raw edges are covered with fancy embroidery stitches.

EMBROIDERY FLOSS
Sewing thread in 6 strands, which can be split if you want to use just 3 strands. It comes in lots of colors.

ENGLISH PATCHWORK
Fabric is basted over paper templates. When sewn together, the paper is removed.

FABRIC CRAYONS
Special crayons that are fixed and washable after ironing.

FLEECE
Fabric made from fluffy synthetic material. It is warm and won't fray.

FUSIBLE BONDING WEB
A paper with thin glue on one side that is ironed to fabric to make it sticky.

GRAIN
The direction of the fabric's woven fibers.

HEM
The finished edge—usually made by folding a raw edge over twice, then stitching down with a hemstitch.

HEXAGON
A six-sided geometric shape used in patchwork.

PATCHES
Pieces of cut-up fabric used to make patchwork.

PATCHWORK
Joining fabric patches or pieces of fabric to form a pattern.

PENTAGON
A five-sided patchwork geometric shape.

PINKING SHEARS
Scissors with a jagged edge, which make a zigzag-shaped edge.

QUILTING
Stitching through three layers of fabric, usually the top, the batting, and the backing fabric.

QUILTING BEE
A group of people working together on the same quilt.

QUILTING IN THE DITCH
Quilting in which the quilting lines are next to the seams.

QUILTING NEEDLE
A short, fine needle for making tiny stitches.

RUNNING STITCH
A straight stitch used for joining seams and quilting.

SASHING
Strips of fabric used to separate and frame quilt blocks.

STUFFING
Soft fabric like cotton balls or puffed-out batting used for stuffing trapunto work.

TEMPLATE
An accurate, full-sized design used as a tracing and cutting guide. Can be made from plastic or cardboard.

TEMPLATE PLASTIC
A see-through plastic sheet ideal for making templates.

TRAPUNTO
A quilting technique in which extra stuffing is added to small areas of the work.

VELCRO
A type of fastening tape. One side has small plastic grips and the other is fluffy, so that when the two join, they stick together.

VOILE
A thin, transparent fabric.

WATER SOLUBLE INK PEN
A pen used for marking quilting lines. The ink fades away when sponged with water.

ZIGZAG STITCH
A basic machine stitch that sews in a zigzag pattern.

Index

Credits

Quarto would like to thank Hettie Reatchlous, Tattie Reatchlous, Ayse Khan, Kay O'Doherty, Daisy Savory, Rosie Froud, and Brodie Clark for modeling the projects in this book.

All photographs and illustrations are the copyright of Quarto Publishing plc. While every effort has been made to credit contributors, Quarto would like to apologize should there have been any omissions or errors.

Author's acknowledgment

The author would like to thank Miriam Edwards and the girls of the Young Quilters of the Quilters Guild of The British Isles for the use of the Elephant quilt.

Thanks also to her grandaughters, Zoë and Alice Stapleton, for the cushion pictures in Project 6, and to Laurence and Alistair Smith for the use of their hands for the snuggle rug in Project 9.